ROOM IN OUR
HEARTS
ROOM IN OUR
HOME

ROOM IN OUR HEARTS ROOM IN OUR HOME

MONROE and JOE ANN BALLARD
with KATHERINE BARRETT

impact
books

ROOM IN OUR HEARTS, ROOM IN OUR HOME. © Copyright 1979 by IMPACT BOOKS, a division of The Benson Company. All rights reserved. Printed in the United States of America. No part of this book may be used or reproduced in any manner whatsoever without written permission, except in the case of brief quotations embodied in critical articles or reviews. For information, write: IMPACT BOOKS, The Benson Company, 365 Great Circle Road, Nashville, Tennessee 37228.

MO601

ISBN 0-914850-80-6

Library of Congress Catalog Card Number 79-90249

TO
Seth Ballard, Sr.
and
DeLoach Benjamin
our fathers, now deceased,
who taught us to
"do right,
work hard,
and put God and family first."

CONTENTS

PART ONE

THE HOUSE THAT KEEPS ON GROWING

PART TWO

HOW TO GO ABOUT DOING GOOD

WELCOME . . .

"Are you sure we can't offer you a coat from our clothes closet?" Joe Ann Ballard watched me with concern as I shivered in the front seat of her tan '73 Maverick. It was a freezing January afternoon, and my light jacket afforded little protection against the icy Memphis winds.

I had no coat that first day when I met Monroe and Joe Ann Ballard. But, unlike most of their young friends, I was coatless through my own thoughtlessness—not because of deprivation or poverty. I had come from New York City to interview the Ballards for a *Family Circle* magazine article and had left my warmest winter clothes at home.

The story I was researching was to focus on a young black couple who have served as surrogate parents to hundreds of ghetto children. But I soon found the Ballards' work encompasses all ages and all levels of society. In the twelve years of their marriage, Monroe and Joe Ann have befriended literally thousands— including this shivering magazine writer, a city official with troubled kids, a child craving a balanced diet of food and love, a young woman needing a temporary home and direction for her life.

Every attempt at defining what the Ballards do for people ends in a list. The 41-year-old schoolteacher and his 35-year-old wife:

1. encourage dozens of young people to attend college—and help them secure financial aid.
2. find hundreds of jobs for the unemployed.
3. provide children with Sunday dinners, clothes, weekend activities, spiritual guidance, and love.
4. host an annual Christmas party for over two hundred needy youngsters.
5. act as a liaison between the poor and bureaucracies.
6. expand their family to include "foster" daughters who live, eat, and worship in their home for an indefinite period of time.

I could go on, but that is the purpose of our book. Part One describes the Ballards' unique lifestyle and tells why they have chosen to live this way. The questions and answers in Part Two are designed to provide an easy reference for the reader and give practical suggestions on how to become more involved with the needs of people around us.

As I have come to know the Ballards well, I am constantly amazed at the number of activities they are able to fit into each day. Even with the demands of three children of their own and two full-time jobs, they seem to have unlimited time to solve the problems and meet the needs of strangers.

They can do it, they tell me, because they decided long ago that the comfortable trappings of middle-class life and leisure are not important to them. The money and time that others spend on houses, cars and vacations are channeled into efforts to relieve some of the suffering they see just down the street from their home.

Why do they do it?

Certainly not for the congratulatory letters that have come from social service officials, the mayor of Memphis, a prominent official from Shelby County, and their congressman.

Certainly not for the awards they have received, though the awards have been numerous—the Congressional Community Service Award (1978); the Optimist Citizen of the Year Award (1977); the Memphis Newspaper Guild Citizen of the Year Award (1977); and, most recently, a two-month "Salute to Mr. and Mrs. Ballard" from the Memphis chapter of Operation P.U.S.H.

Monroe and Joe Ann live their lives for others because they believe that it is truly "more blessed to give than to receive."

For two years I covered the human services beat as a reporter for *The Commercial Appeal* in Memphis. During that time I marveled at the large number of social service agencies and the difficulty that most of them face in providing anything more than short-term, stopgap help. They can offer food, better housing, money, job training, and even counseling, but the roots of poverty are deeply embedded in the family life and attitudes of the poor.

Monroe and Joe Ann generously share their possessions, but more importantly, they share themselves. Because they invite young people to come into their home to live with them and abide by their rules and principles, they are able to make an impact that no institution can match.

I am white and they are black. I am Jewish and they

are Christian. I come from New York City. Their roots are deep in Mississippi. Such differences only highlight the universality of the Ballards' message. They have been an example and an inspiration to me, as I believe they will be to all who read their story.

Katherine Barrett
New York City
September, 1979

PART ONE

THE HOUSE THAT
KEEPS ON GROWING

"It's just an awful situation, Monroe," Joe Ann said sorrowfully. "There's nothing worse than being in a home where you're not wanted. Nothing at all . . ." She paused a moment, then added hopefully, "But we have plenty of room in our home . . ."

*Inasmuch as ye have done it unto
one of the least of these my brethren,
ye have done it unto me.*

MATTHEW 25:40

1

PLENTY OF ROOM

Graduation exercises began that steaming, cloudless day in June with the traditional "Pomp and Circumstance" march. Cameras clicked and babies cried as graduating seniors, perspiring under their black gowns, filed to their seats. Proud parents in the decorated gym fanned themselves with programs and scanned the rows of capped heads for their children.

"Look, Mama," whispered one little girl, tugging at the long, flower-print sleeve of her mother's dress. "There's Karice now. See how she's smiling? Oh, and look. There's Anna too. Her cap's on crooked." Eleven-year-old Ephie Ballard suppressed a giggle and pointed toward the procession of graduates. Her mother, Joe Ann, gently lifted her sleeping, three-year-old son from her lap and placed him in his Daddy's arms. She reached for her movie camera and stood up. Tiptoeing swiftly past the purple and white "Welcome, Alumni" signs, Joe Ann hurried to the front of the large room, where she could get clear shots of the graduates. Karice, a tall, attractive black girl, *was* smiling as if she couldn't stop, twisting her ring nervously as she always did when excited.·

Anna, her sister, seemed to be poised and calm. Joe Ann noticed that she had gained some weight during her college years. She had a healthy glow, and her large, dark eyes were glistening as they never had before.

15

The movie camera whirred as Joe Ann Ballard panned slowly over the orchestra, the potted palms that dotted the stage, her graduating "daughters," and the rest of the family sitting in the audience—an island of black faces in a sea of white. Little Monroe Jr. had awakened and was sleepily waving to the camera. Joe Ann's tall, handsome husband, Monroe, was listening intently to the music. The little girls, Ephie and Linda, dangled their feet off the chairs and squirmed impatiently. And the twenty-year-old twins, Lisa and Allison, whispered quietly to each other. It was a loving, close-knit family. *What a shame*, thought Joe Ann as her lips curled into a light-hearted smile, *what a shame that some of the other two hundred and fifty children couldn't be here to enjoy this occasion.*

The proud mother turned off the camera. The procession ended, and the commencement speaker rose to offer his solemn address over the hum of two electric fans, which served only to stir the warm, humid air in the packed gymnasium.

Still standing, Joe Ann tried to concentrate on the speaker's words, but her mind wandered as she looked at Karice and Anna. There would be so much to do when the family returned home to Memphis. She would need to see that the two college graduates got jobs. Another "daughter," Winnie, was pregnant and must be taken to the doctor. The Ballards had planned a clothes giveaway at their church on the following Saturday. And Lisa, one of the twins, would need help preparing for her high school equivalency test. A typical week. It was difficult for most people to believe all that Joe Ann and her husband accomplished in that time.

She remembered with amusement a conversation earlier that day. She and Anna had been talking beside a willow tree on the clover-covered lawn of the Nashville college, when a lanky, bald administrator stopped to shake her hand. "You've got some mighty fine daughters, Mrs. Ballard. But you certainly don't look old enough to have college-age children."

Joe Ann smiled. "Oh, yes. And we've already married two of our older daughters. Another is a missionary. One teaches school. Three others are still in college . . ."

The man scratched his head. "But you can't be more than thirty-five."

"Actually, I'm thirty-four," Joe Ann laughed. "My husband and I have just been very busy."

It was true that in their twelve years of marriage, Joe Ann and Monroe Ballard had been substitute parents to hundreds of teenagers and children—in addition to their own three. Some, like Karice, Anna, and the twins, had actually lived with the couple. Others regularly came to dinner, spent weekends, sought advice, received clothes, got help in finding jobs—and in discovering themselves.

In the gym, Joe Ann turned again to watch the smiling, attentive faces of Karice and Anna. Since she and Monroe had offered the girls a home five years before, they had changed a great deal. Observing their happiness, she couldn't help thinking of the discouragement that had plagued them for so many years. The devastating words of thoughtless relatives echoed in her mind.

"They'll never amount to anything."

"They're not college material."

"Why can't lazy, good-for-nothing girls like them get jobs?"

The girls' real family had been wrong. So wrong. Happily, that was all over now.

A crescendo in the commencement speaker's voice roused Joe Ann from her reverie. He was coming to the end of the speech, exhorting the members of the graduating class to lead good, wholesome, truth- seeking lives. "May you never be diverted from the course of right by favors and bribes," he boomed. "May you not be driven by selfish ambition."

Joe Ann readied her camera for the moment when her daughters would walk forward to receive their college diplomas. She listened to the endless string of names that came before theirs: *Jan Norman, Elsa Norris, Donald Oakley, Teddy O'Hara* —then finally, *Anna and Karice Phillips.* The camera whirred once again as the girls, in turn, shook the college president's hand.

They made it, thought Joe Ann, *in spite of the discouragement; in spite of the doomsayers and doubting Thomases.*

When the last proud graduate had received his diploma and the benediction was given, the Ballards headed out to the lush, green campus. Still in their black caps and gowns, Karice and Anna posed for pictures, embraced each other, and joked happily with their family.

Joe Ann pictured them as they had appeared five years before . . . They arrived at the door one rainy day in May, clutching bulging shopping bags and two small, dilapidated suitcases. Anna's eyes looked hollow and vacant, and Karice was so painfully shy that the Ballards almost questioned whether she could speak at all.

Joe Ann and Monroe had agreed to take these two "instant daughters" several days before, following a visit from the girls' older sister. The tall, nervous woman had taken care of them since their mother's death. Since the girls had been Monroe's students, she had sought them out in a state of exhausted desperation.

"I'll tell you, Joe Ann," the sister began as she sipped a cup of coffee at the kitchen table. "Those two girls will never amount to anything. Sometimes, I think they're just plain stupid.

"Why, Anna is past eighteen, and Karice is coming up on her eighteenth birthday, but are they trying to find jobs? No. Are they trying to help around the house? No. They just sit around all day and watch television."

A bitter litany of complaints followed. She had five children of her own. How could she be expected to take care of those big lazy girls too? It was ruining her marriage. Her sisters wouldn't even greet their brother-in-law when he came home from work. When you asked them a question, they refused to answer. They were eating so much that the family would end up in the poorhouse. And they weren't even grateful for what she was doing for them.

Joe Ann listened sympathetically to her friend, but she knew she wasn't hearing all the story. As a teacher's aide in high school, she had gotten to know Anna. In bits and pieces, she had learned some of the grim facts about Anna's early life.

Anna and Karice were the youngest in a poor Arkansas family of twelve children. Their father, a farmer who could barely feed his family, died before they were in first grade, leaving their mother to continue the frantic struggle for survival. Shortly afterwards, she moved to Memphis, Tennessee. But in the black ghetto of a racially divided city, her hopes of a better life for her children dissolved. Pounding the pavement day after day in search of a job brought her nothing but sore feet. Their meager supply of food just wouldn't stretch far enough, and she began to fear the influences of the hot, humid city, where so many hopeless, unemployed black men stood listlessly on street corners and so many youths turned to petty crime.

Confused and desperate, she sent some of the children to stay with relatives. While Anna remained in Memphis, Karice went to live with an aunt, who took advantage of the free labor. Between the ages of eleven and fifteen, the young girl spent her time cooking on a wood-burning stove, chopping wood, and picking cotton. Finally she rejoined her sister Anna in Memphis. About a year later, their mother died and the girls become unwanted guests in the home of their sister.

Joe Ann knew that in many ways the older sister's complaints were true. The girls *did* come home from high school, plop themselves down on the ragged, green couch, turn on the television, and slouch there for hours. If the sister didn't stop them, they would snack constantly, sleep until noon on weekends, and play the radio at night when the rest of the family was trying to sleep. But she could sympathize with Karice and Anna too. They felt unwanted. It was a miserable life. So they escaped into the television and their own cold, defensive silence. As deeply as their sister resented their ingratitude, they resented her demands. As deeply as she resented them for "eating up all the groceries," they resented her for monitoring their every bite.

"It's just an awful situation, Monroe, "Joe Ann said the evening after their sister's visit. "There's nothing worse than being in a home where you're not wanted. Nothing at all."

The sixth-grade teacher nodded sadly. It was a shame to see those girls destroyed. As Anna's former teacher, he knew she was bright. Karice, too, had a good mind. But lately both girls had retreated into silent shells. Even in church they looked withdrawn and unhappy.

For hours the Ballards sat on the long couch in their simple living room, talking about the situation and what they could do about it. Since their marriage, they had accommodated a string of long-term guests in the house: Monroe's two brothers, a cousin, and Joe Ann's foster mother, who lived there still. They wondered. With two children of their own and with both of them working full-time, would they be able to muster the time, money, and energy to take in two neglected girls?

It didn't take long for them to come up with the answer. Of course. If they had the time, money, and energy to host an annual Christmas party for two hundred neighborhood youngsters; to collect clothing and damaged goods from stores to give to the poor; to take children to church and pay for their Sunday dinners; to invite dozens of young people into their home every week; to help these same young people find jobs and scholarships, they certainly could find the time, money, and energy to care for two new daughters.

Soon the conversation took a practical turn. "We have those bedrooms in the attic that would do fine for the Phillips girls," Monroe said. "I can build closets for them, and I've been meaning to install a bathroom up there anyway."

"I really believe that both girls are college material," Joe Ann told her husband. "Perhaps your brother, Sylvester, can help them get scholarships at the college in Nashville where he's a student. Then they could stay here on vacations."

"What about clothes?" Monroe asked, jotting notes on a small pad. "We'll have to see about that too. Have you noticed what those girls have been wearing to church? I don't believe they have winter coats."

So the conversation went as dozens of others had gone before. Instead of idly lamenting the plight of the girls, the Ballards were ready to take action. They were on the phone with the sister the very next day.

"We have plenty of room here," they told the astonished woman. "We would love to have Karice and Anna come live with us."

If I had one message to give to people,
it would be: Don't give up. You can
make it if you keep on trying.

— KARICE PHILLIPS

2

KARICE AND ANNA

After the graduates had said their last bubbly good-byes to college friends, the Ballard family climbed into their second-hand motor home and started for Memphis.

Buzzing along Interstate 40, Karice relaxed and listened to the others harmonizing in a gospel song. There was always music in the Ballard family. But—because she and Joe Ann couldn't keep the beat or sing in harmony, they provided an appreciative audience for the others.

Karice had different interests. She glanced at the biology textbooks that she had carefully tied and placed on the seat cushion that morning. She had decided that she wanted to return to school for her master's degree in science some day. Perhaps, in the field of medicine, she, too, could help others. Now, staring absently at the passing trees and signs, she was filled with conflicting emotions—sadness at leaving the school and friends she loved; apprehension at facing the outside world again; happiness at having finished college; wonder, immense wonder, at actually having graduated; gratitude for the couple who had made it all possible.

She felt a hand shaking her shoulder. "What are you doing, girl?" Lisa asked. "Thinking about some boyfriend you're leaving behind?"

Karice smiled at her foster sister. Lisa was always thinking about boys, always giggling and teasing. Even at twenty, she had a lot of growing up to do.

23

"No, I wasn't thinking about a boy. I was thinking about Joe Ann and Monroe."

"Oooh. They made me so mad last week," Lisa cried in mock anger. "They didn't want me to go to that Libertyland place with Todd because they say he's a bad influence. They say, 'Lisa, you don't need a man within a hundred miles right now.' "

Karice laughed in agreement. By the age of fifteen, Lisa had borne her first child. Two more followed in the next two years. The unhappy girl had been taken into the Ballard family just three weeks after she had lost all three children to the welfare department. Stubborn and resentful, Lisa had settled into the Ballard home. During the year she had been with them, her disposition had improved, even though she was as impetuous as ever. Karice tugged her hair affectionately and returned to her thoughts.

Sometimes she just couldn't understand how her foster parents handled all the difficult situations they encountered. Their home was filled with troubled teenagers. No matter how many there were, there always seemed to be room for more.

Karice remembered how astonished she had been in the months after she and Anna had moved into the red brick home. Of course, it didn't take much to surprise her at first—meals that continued until you were full, no excessive chores, a room of her own. All that was a shock. Then there were the younger teenagers who gathered in droves around the house on weekends. How did Joe Ann and Monroe have the energy, the time, and the patience to handle those kids?

Karice thought of big, gangly Tony, the thirteen-year-old boy who had never used silverware before he came to the Ballards' for Sunday dinner. On his first visit, Joe Ann had prepared baked ham, black-eyed peas, and turnip greens—hardly the food you would eat with your hands. But Tony put his fingers in everything. Later the boy told Monroe he had rarely eaten at a table with other people and had never used a fork. In fact he had seldom eaten a real meal at all— surviving, instead, on cookies and snacks.

"Eating works better if you do it like this," Monroe had said gently but firmly, showing the youth how to use the different utensils. He was so matter-of-fact and direct that the boy learned quickly, without embarrassment. After a couple of months, Tony had even become a good cook himself.

Then there was Lynn, a fifteen-year-old "swinger," who wore dresses that were too tight and too short. She hung around the corner store on the Ballards' block. One day Joe Ann stopped to invite her to church.

"You're asking *her?*" Anna had been aghast. The girl looked like a tramp. She wore her hair in an uneven afro and her nails were usually painted with an outlandish shade of polish. One week it would be purple; the next week, green.

But Joe Ann, who never wore any makeup herself, was not easily discouraged. It wasn't long before she had persuaded the girl to visit on weekends and spend the night in one of the empty attic bedrooms. The Ballards encouraged her to wear more suitable clothes and give up her nail polish. They helped her select several new dresses and shoes from a load of damaged goods that had been donated by a nearby department store.

That was a start. Unfortunately, the girl's problems went deeper—far deeper—than that. One Saturday evening when she was staying overnight, Karice stopped by her bedroom. Lynn was sitting on the bed, combing her hair with a comb that had vanished from Joe Ann's night table the week before. Karice was outraged. "That's Mrs. Ballard's comb!"

"It is not."

"Of course it is."

"I bought it myself."

"You did not."

As it turned out, Karice was right. That night, Joe Ann had a long talk with Lynn, who admitted that she had taken the comb.

Sullen and ashamed, Lynn heard Joe Ann repeat words that had never impressed her before: "Stealing is wrong," the young mother explained earnestly. "The Bible says, 'Thou shalt not steal.' "

Lynn dropped her head. Then she heard a strange, new message from Joe Ann.

"If you need a comb or *anything else*, you don't have to take it, Lynn. All you have to do is ask."

The following weekend, Joe Ann took Lynn shopping and bought her a comb of her own. The message had found its mark: When people share, there is no need for stealing.

Karice remembered that she, too, had once been a problem for the Ballards. In the beginning she and her sister, Anna, had been so scared, so shy, so defensive. Looking back, she felt sorry for Joe Ann and Monroe. But at the time, she was feeling sorry for only one person in the world—herself.

Her hands had been shaking so hard that she could barely hold her suitcase that day five years ago when she and Anna had moved in. Powerless and passive, she stood in the doorway, watching indifferently as Monroe and Joe Ann tried to make the sisters feel at home.

"Welcome, girls. We're so pleased to have you. Let

me help you with those bags, Miss Karice." Mr. Ballard's cheerful bass voice seemed to come from a great distance. She watched silently as he picked up her few possessions and carried them up the narrow stairs to the attic room.

Mrs. Ballard and Anna were talking, though Karice could hear that the older woman was making most of the conversation. The eighteen-year-old girl stared around the living room, which was so much lighter, neater, and larger then the one in her sister's house. She spied six-year-old Ephie peeking at her from the dining room entrance. She noticed the piano in the corner of the room and dozens of Mother's Day cards on the mantel under a large clock.

"Are you hungry, girls? Would you like a bite to eat first, or would you rather see your room upstairs?"

She shrugged her shoulders at the tall, slightly stout woman, whose large brown eyes focused on her with kind concern.

Later, during a dinner of chicken, sweet potatoes, and turnip greens, the couple had talked merrily with each other, their little daughters, and the new guests. Karice and Anna had remained silent, sometimes not answering them at all, sometimes muttering a word or two in reply. But the sisters had eaten more than they ever remembered. They watched in amazement as Mr. Ballard kept refilling their plates.

Looking back on those early weeks in the Ballard home, Karice wondered how her foster parents had remained so positive.

"Didn't you ever get annoyed with us for being so spooky?" she had once asked Joe Ann.

"No. We hoped you'd come out of it."

"But how could you bear to keep talking when no one answered? How could you *not* get mad?"

Joe Ann laughed. "We knew you felt there were too many people mad at you already. We thought we'd try something different."

The plan had worked. In a short while, Karice and Anna began to feel at home. They started to participate in the activities of the household. They began to feel loved for the first time in a very long time. Suddenly even dreams of college no longer seemed impossible. In this remarkable house, anything was possible . . . if only you tried.

In fact, just about everyone comes away from the Ballards' house feeling differently, though they are not always aware of the subtle changes taking place. Joe Ann and Monroe are always teaching something, but every lesson comes indirectly—from their own consistent living. Monroe, a slow learner as a child, is forever encouraging other students. "If I could do it, anybody can," he insists. Joe Ann, raised in a foster home herself, gains instant rapport with children and teenagers who have been abandoned by their natural parents.

Both husband and wife are eager to share what they have learned as well as their material possessions. They seem to know instinctively what each young visitor needs. Sixteen-year-old Eric Wells needs a substitute father who will teach him how to work. His seventeen-year-old friend Tom, a white youth, needs help in controlling his volatile temper. Like Karice, seventeen-year-old Winnie needed care and some financial support after the death of her mother. Judy, Sandy and Donna, three teenage sisters, are spending weekends at the house now. They are learning about home management and, of course, about the Ballards' real specialty—giving.

Aren't they something. Aren't they just something,

thought Karice fondly. She glanced toward the front of the van. Her foster parents were speaking in hushed tones over the sleeping form of their son on the blanket between them. Her sisters, feeling the effects of the day's excitement and the rhythmic hum of the wheels, stretched drowsily.

With the deepening night, silence settled over the little group, homeward-bound. Karice had never felt such peace, such contentment. This had been a good day. She was ready for tomorrow, after all.

*The Ballards were the only ones who
ever did anything for my sister and me.
Only Joe Ann and Monroe Ballard could
have loved the people we were.*

3

—ALISON EVERETT

LISA AND ALISON

For Lisa and Alison, the Ballards' two other "foster" daughters, attending a college graduation was a first — an experience far removed from any they had ever known on the streets of South Memphis. The twins had lived hard in their twenty years and now, in the warmth of a real family, they were embarrassed to talk about what they had been through—drugs, loose living, illegitimate babies, alcohol, a squalid childhood. Now those day seemed a world, a lifetime, away.

But sometimes Lisa still had nightmares about those early years. In her dreams she could see the heavily carved desk in her second-grade classroom.

As she bent over her work, classmates avoided her.

"Phew, you stink," one little boy held his nose pointedly. Another chimed in, "Lisa lives in a sewer. Lisa lives in a sewer." Soon the whole class joined in the chorus, which swelled to a frightening intensity. Awakening abruptly, she would lie trembling, her heart pounding in shame and fear. The childhood chants left their scars, and even the teachers chose subtle ways to humiliate her.

"We'd better open the window in here," one squarish, gray-haired educator said, winking at Lisa's classmates.

Another sent notes home to her mother. "Dear Mrs. Everett," they read, "Your daughter is offensive to the class and must be bathed." Lisa's mother only chuckled, tossed the note aside, and took another swig from her liquor bottle.

31

"Why don't you bathe, Lisa?" she yelled.

It was a joke . . . of sorts. The water and electricity were almost always turned off. The utility money had been spent to buy liquor.

The two girls carried other bitter memories of those years. On a bleak, drizzly night when they were nine, their mother marched them to the cafe where their father was drinking away his weekly paycheck. The couple had separated a short time before. Mrs. Everett berated her daughters as they trudged along behind her on the broken street.

"You girls is ugly. How'd you come to be my kids? Hey, can't you move them bodies any faster? I ain't taking care of you no more. You ain't worth foolin' with because you is your Daddy's kids and he ain't worth foolin' with neither."

The words flowed in an unending stream. As Lisa and Alison hurried to keep up with Mama, their tears mingled with the rain on their cheeks. When they reached the cafe, she left them sitting on the curb and went inside. Nearby, a drunk with a bottle of cheap wine leaned against a lamp post. The heavy odor of alcohol clung to his clothing and seemed to envelop the twins too.

The girls listened as their parents yelled obscenities at each other inside the cafe. "I've left your two out on the street. My two are at home," their mother shouted, referring to their brother and sister. Then she stormed out of the cafe and ran down the street alone, leaving the two crying children at the mercy of their father.

Lisa and Alison's problems were just beginning that day at the cafe door. Life continued its bitter assault at the little white house where they lived with their father and aunt after their mother abandoned them. The twins lived in a world populated by drug pushers and prostitutes, alcoholics and thieves. They grew up quickly in that atmosphere—too fast to play or laugh or enjoy childish things.

"Sometimes when my aunt cooked, the grown people and her daughter would eat first," Lisa told Joe Ann years later. "If nothing was left, we just wouldn't eat that day.

"Most people don't know what going hungry is like, but you reach the point where you'll do anything to fill your stomach. You'll steal if you have to, or maybe you'll ask some guy for the money. You'll do just about anything to survive.

"We never did have enough food to eat or clothes to wear. And nobody ever told us how to act. There are certain things a child should learn when he's growing up—like how to comb his hair, take a bath, change his clothes. You shouldn't get to be sixteen years old without knowing what it's like to take a bath."

Both girls wanted to escape—but how? For Lisa the answer was men. At the age of fifteen, she met an older man who was "cute and bright, with a good afro." He was the first of many. Out of these relationships came babies—three adorable children whom Lisa couldn't care for. After all, she was only a child herself.

While Lisa was searching for security, her sister Alison was moved to a foster home by the welfare department. This turned out to be another tragic experience.

Her new "mother" was a scowling, harsh matron who pulled Alison's hair, shouted insults, and made her slave in the kitchen.

"Your Mama left you. Your Daddy didn't want you,

and if you give me any talk, I'll throw you out too, you lazy thing," the woman threatened.

"Stop eating so much. Don't you think you're fat enough already? The government doesn't pay us to feed pigs like you."

In that atmosphere, the unruly, unkempt Alison became more rebellious. She ran away, ended up in another foster home, then ran away again.

For both twins, the future seemed bleak, almost hopeless. But that was before Monroe and Joe Ann.

When the Ballards first met them, Lisa and Alison were twelve years old. They came to church one winter Sunday, shivering under their ragged housecoats. Joe Ann and Monroe invited the twins to visit them on weekends, gave them better clothes, and tried to teach them a better life. It wasn't easy. After so much physical and emotional abuse, the girls had shut off their feelings. Their experiences had taught them not to love. They approached life with resentful indifference.

Joe Ann tried to reach them with shopping outings. But it took a lot of love and patience to break through their shells.

"Look at this lovely blue dress, Alison," Joe Ann would say. "Don't you think it would look nice on you?"

"I don't care."

"Well, what about the yellow one? It would be very pretty on you too."

"I don't care."

"Did you say you needed shoes?"

"I don't care."

Even at the Christmas party—held every year at their home or a local restaurant—Monroe and Joe Ann watched Lisa and Alison unwrap presents with sullen indifference.

Later the twins discussed the day's activities. "What kind of party was that?" Lisa asked her sister. "There wasn't no dancin' and drinkin'."

"Yeah, it was dull," Alison muttered. "Those folks are squares, you know? They don't let you do nothing fun. Everything is 'No. No. No.' "

After their mother left, the twins had lived without any limits. Since no one cared where they were, they had the freedom to come and go at will, do what they pleased, and hang out wherever they wanted to. This became an accepted way of life for the teenagers.

Grudgingly, they went to the Ballards' home a few times when invited, but they rebelled at the restrictions imposed by a normal home life.

"Wish we could do more for those children," Monroe sighed one day. Joe Ann agreed. She began hinting to the girls that the Ballard house could become their permanent home if they wanted to live there.

Lisa and Alison shrugged the invitation off and continued to live as they pleased. But each remembered the offer a few years later. At different times, when each of the girls was emotionally ready, they reached out for the couple's helping hand.

Alison moved in when she was just over seventeen. Lisa followed two years later, after her babies had been placed for adoption. At ages when most teenagers are leaving the security of their childhood homes, the twins were given the opportunity to discover what a real family is like, and they were now a little more willing to accept the rules in order to enjoy the love and protection they so desperately needed.

Alison was sick of the sordid world of the ghetto. She could no longer tolerate the hypocrisy and indifference of foster parents who took children in just for the money. And she was ready to start making some plans for a better life.

Alison brought up the subject herself after she had been living with the Ballards for a while. "I've decided I want to be a missionary," she announced as she helped Joe Ann with the dishes.

The young girl was wearing a simple blue dress and her face shone with excitement. Joe Ann turned to look at her in surprise. But then she realized she had no reason to be surprised. *Why shouldn't this girl become a missionary?* The idea seemed strange only when Joe Ann closed her eyes and pictured Alison as she had appeared several months before—in tight jeans and a stained T-shirt, her hair in a dirty, long afro.

"I think that's a wonderful idea—just great," Joe Ann smiled. "If you want to go to college, maybe we can help you find a scholarship. Why don't you talk to John when he comes home from vacation next week? You know, he's studying to be a minister."

Alison already knew more than she cared to know about John. He was a member of the Ballards' church, but she remembered him as a skinny, stuck-up know-it-all. In the old days, she and Lisa often teased him unmercifully. *So that's what had become of him.*

"That guy? No thanks. He's just a big baby." Alison wrinkled her nose in disgust.

"Well, never mind about that. I'll talk to your social worker tomorrow and see if she can give us some ideas about financial aid."

The next day, Joe Ann strode across the mall in front of the state office building and pushed through the revolving doors. She was full of plans and eager to get started.

After ten minutes in the packed, noisy waiting room,

Joe Ann was ushered to the desk of Alison's case-worker. She was a thin, well-dressed woman wearing hoop earrings and a tight smile.

"That girl certainly has given us a lot of trouble, Mrs. Ballard. I take my hat off to you for putting up with her. She seems like a very difficult girl." The social worker looked sympathetically at Joe Ann, who got right to the point.

"Alison wants to be a missionary. I wonder if we could get her some kind of grant to help her through school."

"A missionary? That *is* something, isn't it?"

"Can you help? Or give me any advice on how to apply for financial aid?"

"I'm sorry, but our responsibility for Alison has ended. Her eighteenth birthday is only a month away. Frankly, Mrs. Ballard, I wouldn't waste my time with her. We've tried and tried to help that girl, but none of it did any good. We just don't feel that Alison is a good investment."

Not a good investment? Joe Ann's head reeled as she walked to her car. *That's looking at a person as nothing more than a dollar mark. You ought to help people because they need it — not because they can return everything you give them, plus interest.*

But her dejection didn't last long. Neither Joe Ann nor Monroe listened to fruitless defeatist talk like that. If Alison wanted to go to college, they would do everything possible to see that she went.

With John's help and Joe Ann's persistence, Alison was on her way within a few months to the Nazarene Bible College in Colorado Springs, Colorado. She left with piles of donated clothing, sheets, bathroom supplies, and notebooks which Joe Ann had rounded up from churches in the community. She knew from experience that most people will give if presented with a need, so she called churches all over town and told them of Alison's situation.

Alison's college years flew by, with vacation time spent at "home" with the Ballards. They were her family now—the ones who sent extra spending money when they could spare it, wrote her newsy letters of family happenings, and eagerly accepted her occasional long-distance collect calls "just to see how everybody's doin'."

And she did change her opinion of John . . .

After graduation, nine years after she had been deserted by her "real" mother, Alison gazed at herself in the mirror of the Ballard home in disbelief. The full skirt of her lacy, white dress was etched with delicate, white daisies. A froth of net falling from a crown of daisies framed her glowing face. In a few hours, Monroe Ballard—more of a father to her than her own had ever been—would escort her down the aisle of Memphis South Church of the Nazarene to "give her away" to a young minister, her husband-to-be—John!

In all her wildest dreams, she had never believed she would have a wedding like this—complete with a white lace dress, a tiered wedding cake, flowers everywhere, bridesmaids in silver dresses with red and white bouquets.

She arranged her veil. *I'm not so ugly,* she thought as she peered into the mirror. *Why did my mother always say I was ugly?* It had taken Alison a long time to forgive the woman who had abandoned her in front of the cafe so many years before.

She turned as her "foster" father entered the room with a wide smile on his face. "I declare, Miss Alison," he beamed. "You're just about the prettiest thing I ever did see!"

For Alison's twin sister, Lisa, the adjustment was a little tougher.

"It's always hard to get used to something new," Lisa sighed one day as she and her newly married sister sorted clothes together in the Ballard home. "I just don't know if I can take it anymore."

"You know that rules are necessary," said Alison. "Without them, there is nothing but chaos."

Lisa frowned. "The old way, we stayed out as long as we wanted and came home when we pleased. Sometimes, I just feel like going back."

"You'll make it," Alison interrupted, encouraging her sister with a hug. "I never dreamed I'd marry a preacher. You know what he tells me? He says, 'You look the same, but you're a different person than you used to be.' I praise the Lord for that. You should too. No one except Joe Ann and Monroe Ballard could have loved the people we were."

The Ballards were wise enough to realize that Lisa needed limits. From the very beginning they let her know that they loved her too much to let her do exactly as she pleased. They were consistent and persistent in the rules they set up for her behavior.

"Why are you always checking up on me?" Lisa whined after a lecture on coming home late. "So what if I'm a little late. Why is it such a big deal?"

"No, I don't want to help you with the dishes," she retorted. "Do your own dishes."

"It's *my* room upstairs," she told Joe Ann one day. "You said so. If I don't want to make my bed, why should I? I've taken care of myself for a long time and I don't need you telling me what to do."

"We told you when you came here that you would have to follow certain rules," Joe Ann always replied patiently. "Your resistance is just making them harder."

In her bedroom at night, Joe Ann would share with Monroe the thoughts that she had kept hidden during the day.

"That child is giving me fits. I've told her a dozen times to clean up after her bath. But she leaves her clothes on the floor and a big ring in the tub.

"And she can't seem to understand why we worry about her," Joe Ann continued. "She resents it if I ask where she's going. I'm just trying to keep her away from her old friends. She knows they can lead her right back into trouble."

Lisa did know, but she still resented the restrictions life with the Ballards brought. Bright, giggly, and explosive, she seemed to waver between good and bad, between respect and rudeness. But as the days and months went by, she began to change . . . so much so that one day she surprised her new family.

On a hot, summer day she was invited to go to an amusement park with some of her co-workers at her part-time job. Monroe encouraged her.

"Why don't you go, Lisa? You can give us a report on the new rides."

Anna was stretched out on the living room couch, reading and listening. Seven-year-old Linda Ballard was kneeling on the floor nearby, sketching with colored pencils.

"Go on, Lisa. It'll be fun," Anna piped in.

"May I come too?" Linda looked up hopefully.

Lisa stared thoughtfully through the window at the yellow trim on the house next door. "No. I'm not going."

"You scared of the rides?" Linda teased.

Lisa gave her a disgusted look and stormed out of the room, through the kitchen, into the den. Monroe followed. "Something wrong, Lisa?"

"Nah. It's okay."

"I'm a little puzzled. You made such a fuss when we refused to let you go to the amusement park a month or two ago."

"I know." Lisa's eyes darted around the room to cover her embarrassment. "I just don't want to go with those women from work. They've got such filthy mouths and—well, I guess I don't feel right hanging around people who cuss."

Eyebrows raised with wonder, Monroe patted her on the shoulder. "You don't have to be ashamed about that. And you certainly don't have to go if you don't want to."

Monroe and Lisa had other chats that left him optimistic about the girl's future. Although she had dropped out of high school after the birth of her first baby, Monroe encouraged her to go back to school, to try for a high school equivalency diploma, and to think of college.

"Don't ever say *can't*, Lisa," he admonished. "You can graduate if I did. Let me tell you how it was when I was in school.

"My seven brothers and sisters and I went to a tiny school that my own Granddaddy built years ago. Back then, all the children had only one teacher for every course, and they sat in one small room all day.

"The teacher would paddle you if you didn't know the lesson. I tried as hard as I could, but I couldn't read as well as the other students. That teacher was always taking after me with a switch. I started wearing several layers of clothes to school to protect myself from the paddlings."

Lisa giggled, picturing the young Monroe sweating in the classroom under several shirts. Now he was a respected teacher, with a master's degree in special education. "How'd you make it so far?" she asked.

"I just tried and tried, then I tried some more. If I couldn't read my lessons, my Mama would help me memorize them. We'd sit together on the porch and go over the words again and again.

"That's how I learned that anybody can make it," he told Lisa. "There are always people like my Mama who are willing to help if you will just ask. There is no reason to fail, unless you sit around doing nothing."

Teach a child how he should live,
and he will remember it all his life.

—PROVERBS 22:6, TEV

4

MONROE

The lesson that Monroe passed on to Lisa that day was one of many that he learned from his own parents. The simple, steady values of Seth Ballard and his wife, Lucille—their neighborliness, Christian faith, and love for their family—provided the basis for Monroe's lifelong desire to work hard and help others.

"I just can't thank Mama and Daddy enough," Monroe told Joe Ann as they sat on the porch of his parents' tiny house during a summer visit early in their marriage. "They have taught me so much about life and living. Maybe I can pass on to others a little of what they have given me."

Monroe was born in a six-room, weather-blackened frame house in Flora, Mississippi, a rural community about fifteen miles outside of Jackson. He was the third oldest child in a family of eight children. He shared a bed with his brothers and sisters, the hardships of a poor black family, and the wisdom of parents who wanted a better life for their children.

His father, Seth Ballard, was a farmer and community herb doctor, who had gone to college briefly himself. He always stressed the importance of education to his children. Working with his father in the fields, Monroe also learned the dignity and value of labor.

"You sure are a good worker for your age, boy," Seth Ballard told his ten-year-old son one afternoon. Shy and quiet, Monroe beamed at his father and worked harder still, holding tightly to the reins as the mule team team pulled the plow along.

"Tell me about when you were little, Daddy," Monroe begged, though he had heard these stories dozens of times before.

"See here, son? Right where we're plowing. Yes, sir. We lived right around here. See that oak? We used to sit under that tree and your granddaddy would tell us boys how he expected us to grow up to be big, fine, straight men.

" 'Learn to pray,' your Granddaddy would say. 'Get to know the Lord.' "

Monroe's father never worked in silence. He was always teaching his son something.

"You see that leaf, son? Take a few of them and make tea—good strong tea—and it'll cure a headache.

"Remember what this little white flower can do?"

"Cure rheumatism?"

"That's right. I just can't seem to find enough of this plant. Folks have so many aches and pains these days."

Seth Ballard was one of the most respected men around Flora. To make extra money, he would gather sassafras roots, black snake roots, and Devil Shoe-string, then trudge ten to fifteen miles to peddle the herbs.

"Let me tell you this, Monroe," he said one day as they were stringing a long chain of sassafras. "Sometimes, the roads are muddy, and I can't get home 'til late. But I don't mind the work because I'm doin' it for my family. My family is my business. It's my pride. There isn't anything I wouldn't sacrifice for you and the other kids.

"You remember that when you have a family. Your wife and children should come first. Yes, sir. Do right, go straight, and take care of your home."

Even as a child, Monroe realized that providing and caring for eight children wasn't easy. In those days in the South, the white man's word was the law. What chance did a poor black farmer and herb doctor have to provide a comfortable home for his family? Ankle-deep mud hindered transportation on rural roads. Crops were uncertain. His father worked from sunup to sundown many times for $2.00 a day.

But somehow, Monroe's family survived. They had their home, and that was just about everything. On Sunday they would sit outside and listen to a homespun Sunday School lesson. At night, Seth Ballard would tell stories from the Bible as his children sat cross-legged on the wooden floor.

Monroe and his brothers and sisters spent many happy hours playing together outside the house or in the nearby woods. They usually played in teams of two, according to age and their special friendships: The two oldest, Seth Jr. and Rosie Mae; Monroe and Janie; the next two girls, Daisy and Mamie; and the babies, Sammy and Sylvester.

Often the children made their playground in the area next to their mother's flower garden. The beauty and fragrance of the garden drew them like the bees that buzzed about on a summer day. And in the precious moments their Mama could spare from her household duties, they could see her bending over her flowers. In loving concentration, she would pull a stray weed or two, or pinch a dying bloom to make room for more.

As the children grew older, there was always work for them to do. Monroe took on more than his share.

During most of his childhood, he was the only boy at home who was able to work. Seth Jr., four years older, had received a scholarship at a boarding school. The two youngest boys were the babies of the brood. So Monroe learned to feel like the man of the house when his father wasn't around. He took his responsibilities seriously.

"Don't want you fighting with those other children," he said to his little sisters as they ate lunch in the school yard. "You stay with me."

When his mother sent the children to cut wood, he made sure no one got hurt. "Janie, you're holding that axe all wrong," he cautioned. "Let me show you how."

Although he might have been a little bossy at times, Monroe seemed to have a way with the younger children. They respected him and looked up to him.

"Monroe, make us a wagon," the toddlers often begged. "Make us a swing. Make us a see-saw." Monroe could do anything. And he was willing to try. Once, he pleased them with a primitive steam engine made from a cast-off oil pump, then took great care to teach the children how to run it safely.

But sometimes his responsibilities weighed heavily. The summer Monroe was fourteen, he and his father spent weeks fixing up the old house. They painted it, repaired the roof, and added on a room. Monroe installed the new electrical wiring himself.

Several months later, he was playing in the school yard one day when his teacher came looking for him. As she walked toward him, Monroe noticed a note in her hand. Its message was brief but shocking: "Your house has burned down and everything is lost."

He heard the rest of the story in bits and pieces on the way home. One neighbor told him his little sisters had passed her house crying. Another informed him that his three-year-old brother had set fire to the house while his father was napping on the porch and his mother was sewing.

Monroe broke into a run down the dusty dirt road, made a shortcut through some bushes, and stopped in front of what used to be his house. Nothing but ashes. The bushes that used to bloom every spring, and the flowers that had lent their color were gone. Fortunately, no one had been injured in the blaze.

The homeless family moved into the nearby school house that had been vacant for four years. But their crops and water supply were two miles away around the charred remains of the old house. For months, fourteen-year-old Monroe rode his bicycle back and forth every day to get bundles of corn and watermelons for the hogs and to haul water for the family.

This additional work seemed to hasten Monroe's growing sense of responsibility. Physically, he was developing into a tall, muscular, young man. He was obviously proud of the help he could give other people. If tools needed fixing, he repaired them. If his parents needed something from a neighbor, he rode his bike for miles over rough fields and muddy roads.

At the age of seventeen, Monroe went to Piney Woods, a boarding school several miles away. His older sister and brother had already attended this school on scholarships. Later all but one of his younger brothers and sisters would go to the same school.

Away from home, Monroe's family consciousness and desire to help people grew even stronger. As his younger sisters entered the school, he bought them newspapers to read and gave them spending money that he earned cutting hair. Later, as a young soldier, a student, and a beginning teacher, he sent home as much money as he could spare.

During visits back home, he also continued to help his family by plowing, cleaning the woodshed, sawing wood, repairing storage houses, and mending fences. But then, just about all of Seth and Lucille Ballards' children worked hard, helped each other, and sent money home. To them, giving was a family tradition.

More than thirty years have passed since ten-year-old Monroe worked beside his father in the fields. All eight Ballard children have finished college and four have received master's degrees as well. The youngest of the children is now a minister. The oldest is a junior high school principal. In between are three teachers (including Monroe), the founder of a day care center, a PTA president, and an author. They have gone their separate ways, but when they do gather for a family reunion, their voices blend beautifully in a song written in memory of their father:

Daddy lived and walked the Ballard land,
He lived for God and took a Christian stand;
There are a lot of things he said, I heard.
But these are his most important words:
"Do right. Go straight. That's all it takes.
Do right. Go straight. That's all it takes."

To find what we can do, one's
individual place . . . is man's task.

—*FLORENCE NIGHTINGALE*

5

JOE ANN

In the years following World War II, a young farm girl growing up on the rich, hilly land near Lucedale, Mississippi, was learning to be a person who helps others. But her lessons were drawn from a personal tragedy that taught her first what it means to be helped.

Joe Ann Marshall was born into a shattered family—the youngest of three children who drank their first milk from old Coca Cola bottles, and heard their first words from squabbling parents. Fortunately, her life in this environment didn't last long. Three months after Joe Ann was born, her mother and father separated and sent the children to live with a great aunt and uncle.

The dirt and dying grass were covered with auburn leaves when Ora Mae Benjamin heard an unexpected knock on her door one autumn morning. Peeking out, the plump, good-natured woman saw her niece's husband, dressed in fancy clothes. His shiny red sedan looked out of place in front of her unpainted wood-frame house.

He held a baby in his arms. Clinging to his carefully-pressed pants were a little boy and girl. Joe Ann's father wasted no time in getting to the point.

"Bessie and me would like for you to keep the kids for us a few weeks, Ora Mae. Your niece really needs the rest, and we didn't think you'd mind."

49

Ora Mae and her husband, DeLoach, were glad to help. They loved children. It seemed their modest home was always filled with nephews, nieces, and neighborhood children. In fact, with his first wife, who died in the 1920's and later with Ora Mae, DeLoach had already raised forty-five foster children.

The weeks passed, and then the months. Long after autumn had turned to winter, they still heard nothing from Joe Ann's parents. As Ora Mae grew more attached to the three little Marshall children, she stopped wondering and started fearing instead.

"It'll just kill me to give those little ones up," she told her husband, as she cut up flour sacks to make new clothes for the children.

"I know," he nodded, his bad leg stretched out in front of him. "I'm growing right attached to those kids myself."

Soon after that conversation, Mrs. Benjamin answered the phone to hear the shaky, high-pitched voice of Joe Ann's real mother. "Me and Tom are getting a divorce," she said. "I'd like you to raise my babies for me, Aunt Ora."

Although there was never an official adoption, Joe Ann, her sister Lulu, and brother Dyke lived with their foster parents through all their growing-up years. They had a good life and a loving home with the best of clothing that could be made from flour sacks and the best of ham that could be cut from a home-cured hog.

Joe Ann grew into a first-class tomboy. She tagged along after her foster father as he made his rounds on the twelve-acre farm and pecan orchard. A disabled World War I veteran, he was plagued by a bad leg. But he never let that prevent him from swinging Joe Ann off her feet, lifting her to his shoulders, and carrying her for hours.

"What say we all walk to the store?" he would ask the kids on Saturdays.

"Oh, could we?" Joe Ann's eyes grew big with delight, as Dyke and Lulu pulled at his hands.

Even before reaching the store, they could smell the coffee beans and the smoked sausage. As soon as they caught the first whiff, the children raced ahead, battling each other to be first through the creaky door.

"Remember, I earned a quarter," six-year-old Joe Ann reminded her father when he caught up.

"She spent that quarter last week," cried seven-year-old Dyke. "And the week before that and the week before that."

"Well, that's all right," Mr. Benjamin replied. "You children get whatever you want."

Joe Ann looked up at her daddy, who seemed to have the kindest face in the world. All around her were glass jars of lollipops, sourballs, fudge, and button candy. As her father leaned patiently on his wooden cane, she tried to make up her mind, then finally settled on the goodies she had chosen last week— three peppermints, Vienna sausage, and her favorite, orange slices.

There were other good times—lots of them. The three young foster children of the Benjamins spent hours playing baseball, catball, hopscotch, and hide-and-go-seek. At night, they told jokes or listened to Bible stories, while baking potatoes and roasting peanuts in the open fire.

Like Monroe's father, DeLoach Benjamin taught his foster children about honesty, the importance of a good family, and faith in God. Although crippled, he was a hard worker with massive amounts of determination.

"Never give up," he said one sunny afternoon, emphasizing his point by pounding his cane on the ground.

The Marshall children didn't know whether he was talking to them or to himself. They were all struggling together to build a small house. It wasn't an easy task for three children and a crippled man, but they finally completed the job—just the way they managed to work the farm by themselves and save money for a rainy day.

In spite of the warmth of her home and the wisdom of her parents, Joe Ann sometimes mourned her status as a foster child. Like most adopted or foster children, she often wondered what life with her natural parents would be like. Her idealized picture was much brighter than the real thing, as she discovered one week.

Joe Ann was drawing water from her foster parents' old weather-beaten hand pump when a green and white Chevrolet pulled up into the yard. A handsome man wearing a brown bowler hat and a thin, tan tie got out of the car. It was her father.

Joe Ann's week-long visit with him and her stepmother began with an eight-hour ride to his house in Alabama. She thought the trip would never end! Sitting on the clean, white canvas seats of the Chevrolet, she and her brother and sister peered out the windows. They had learned during the first hour to sit quietly without speaking. Their childish play disturbed their father. And during the second hour they learned to keep peppermint sticks in their pockets.

"Just can't stand folks who mess up my car," their father ranted. "Had a man in here the other day who was chewing tobacco. He spat it right out the window. Well, I pulled over to the side of the road, and I said,

'You get out, sir. Don't nobody stay in here who messes up my car.'

"You know what else I hate? Peanut hulls. Yep. People will just drop 'em all over the seats. I almost knocked a man down once for that."

As her father talked, Joe Ann sat as neatly as she could with her hands folded properly in her lap. *That man sure loves his car,* she thought.

When they finally arrived, her father's house turned out to be bigger than her foster parents', but it was cold and forbidding. From the moment she walked in, Joe Ann wanted to go home.

"You'll get used to it," Dyke and Lulu encouraged her. But she didn't.

Their stepmother suffered from throbbing migraine headaches. And she was afraid of her husband. She tried to be pleasant to the three Marshall children, but having them around was obviously a strain.

Feeling bored and unwanted, the young guests met by the woodpile on the third day. They started talking about how they missed their home.

"Why don't we ask if we can start back early?" Dyke wondered.

It sounded reasonable. So the three marched inside the house with their suggestion. Their answer was a resounding no!

Running back to the woodpile, Joe Ann felt an uncontrollable lump in her throat. Her eyes filled with tears. *Maybe they'll never let us go home,* she thought. *What if we have to stay here the rest of our lives?*

Not even Dyke could set Joe Ann's mind at ease. She cried and cried until she was too tired to cry anymore.

As it turned out, her fears were groundless. At the end of the week, the children were on their way home again. But even in the warmth and security of this loving home, Joe Ann had many other tearful moments because she was a foster child.

A pudgy, little boy taunted her on the way home from school one day. "How come you got a different name than your parents, Joe Ann?"

"I don't know," she replied, though she knew perfectly well.

"I hear it's 'cause they're *not* your parents. Your parents didn't even want you."

"That's not true."

"Yes, it is. They probably thought you was too ugly."

Experiences like these could have embittered Joe Ann. Instead, they made her sensitive to the plight of other children who suffered from life's injustices. Inspired by a biography of Florence Nightingale, she determined to devote her life to helping others.

At night she would lie in her cot by the window, listen to the chirping crickets, and think about her past and the future.

That wonderful woman made up her mind to be a nurse and she never let anyone stop her. What was that she wrote in her diary? "I'm going to do it." Well, I'm going to do it too. I won't be a nurse, but I'll help people some other way. And nobody will stop me either . . .

6

ONE + ONE = 250

If Joe Ann and Monroe had advertised for a mate, they could have used the same classified ad: "Wanted: Deeply spiritual mate who loves children, works hard, and doesn't drink, smoke, or curse." Neither was willing to compromise these high standards.

One afternoon nineteen-year-old Monroe was sitting in a lounge at Piney Woods school with his younger sister, Mamie.

"Why don't you introduce yourself to that girl over there," she urged, pointing to an attractive young student.

"Nope. Don't want to."

"You never want to meet anyone. A lot of girls here are dying to go out with you. How are you ever going to find a wife?"

"I'm not worried. The right woman will come along someday." Monroe picked up a newspaper and glanced at it. As far as he was concerned, the conversation was closed. But Mamie persisted.

"What's wrong with that girl over there? She's pretty, and I think she likes you."

Monroe looked up at his sister impatiently. "Look at her slip. It's hanging 'way below her dress. I wouldn't want to go out with her."

Meanwhile, Joe Ann had developed some similar standards of her own. In fact, she had worked out a profile of her husband when she was only sixteen. In the back of her Bible, she listed the requirements for her future partner. Some were childish—like the requirement for someone tall and handsome. But others provided insights into the kind of life she planned to lead. No nicotine or alcohol would ever enter her house. No money would be spent on fancy clothes and frivolous pleasures. She wanted a man of faith who was a good provider and who loved children.

As she grew into an attractive young woman, she dated many different men, none of whom seemed just right.

One suitor at Prentiss, Mississippi Junior College was tall and handsome. But when she dated him, she often smelled alcohol on his breath. Another young man called on her in a fancy new tux. Instead of being charmed, she was turned off by his extravagance.

"I don't need anyone who spends all that money on clothes," she told a friend. "That's not what I want out of life."

At Prentiss, and later when she attended the Nazarene Bible College near Charleston, West Virginia, Joe Ann dressed simply in attractive jumpers, skirts and blouses, or wool suits. Her hair was short and curly; her eyes bright and intense. With her pretty face wearing its customary smile, Joe Ann charmed everyone she met. But everyone knew she had set some mighty high standards for a husband.

When other young women in her dorm seemed puzzled by her pickiness, she explained, "If someone isn't neat and clean on a date, he probably won't be clean around the house. If he isn't concerned about values now, he probably wouldn't be concerned after we married."

As it turned out, it wasn't an advertisement that brought Monroe and Joe Ann together, but some good, old-fashioned matchmaking.

After graduating from Bible college, Joe Ann moved to Memphis to work with the Memphis South Church of the Nazarene. While visiting a sick church member one day, she received some valuable advice.

"I hear there are some interesting young men at the Holiness church." The ailing woman's voice crackled with enthusiasm. "Fetch my purse, dear. I have a name written down somewhere. Here it is: 'Monroe Ballard.' " She winked at Joe Ann as she handed her the slip of paper. "If I were you, I'd check into this."

Joe Ann did, but her first dates with Monroe weren't very promising. His sunglasses were so dark that they hid his eyes completely. Because of the reflected sunlight, she had to blink and turn away. *Oooh . . . those are awful,* she thought. *Who does he think he is—Ray Charles?*

Shy as usual, Monroe said little to erase her impression that he was a "far-out" guy. He was not one to force himself upon people. He preferred to let a relationship develop at a slow, natural pace.

As the months passed, other church members asked Joe Ann out and Monroe dated other women, but the young couple was often thrown together by their work and common interests. She was directing the Sunday School at the Nazarene church, while he was Sunday School superintendent at a nearby Holiness church. They began to realize that their rigorous requirements for mates seemed to match. Several months after their first meeting, they began to talk about marriage.

"I think we'll do well together," Monroe told his future bride. "We've developed a real good fellowship through our work at the churches. A husband and wife should know how to work together."

Monroe was not one to rush into things, but he had a deep feeling that the match was right. The woman he loved was a hard worker but a home-centered person as well; a generous giver who could also be thrifty; a neat dresser but not fancy or frivolous. Most important of all, Joe Ann had high standards of her own. She wouldn't have to adjust to his own exacting requirements.

He remembered how his mother had warned him when he was a teenager: "When you pick your wife, Monroe, pick right. You can't raise a woman over again. What you marry is what you'll get."

No. There won't be any problems with Joe Ann, he thought. *I guess I like her just the way she is.*

It was early November. The morning of the wedding dawned clear and cold. When Monroe's whole family drove to Lucedale, Mississippi, for the big event, they found Joe Ann's hometown abuzz.

"Why, there ain't been a weddin' in our church for nigh on fifty years," an old man explained as he leaned against a maple tree in the churchyard. "All them other young folks find someplace else to go, I reckon. But that Marshall girl—she come back home."

At her foster parents' old wood frame house, Joe Ann tried on her wedding dress. The lace collar looked extra white against her dark skin and the satin skirt flowed gracefully over her legs.

"You look beautiful, Joe Ann," said Mrs. Benjamin, adjusting the crown and veil on her daughter's short hair. A seamstress by trade, she had made the dress herself for only nine dollars, cutting and sewing it lovingly in the cool, damp evenings.

The whole town was invited to the ceremony. About five hundred people crammed into the church or waited outside as the young couple said their vows.

Standing in front of the altar, Joe Ann and Monroe could not foresee what the future held for them, or that this union would mean hope for so many homeless youngsters. That would come later. For the moment—

and perhaps for the only time in their lives—they were completely absorbed in each other.

Joe Ann and Monroe moved into their first apartment a week later. Tiny but clean, it was located on one of the run-down streets of North Memphis. Scanning her new home, Joe Ann realized that it needed a lot of work. Some former tenants had left a big bed right in the middle of the kitchen. It had no bathroom, no curtains, and no heat. But they did have a cooperative landlord, who helped Monroe install a private bathroom and solve the heat problem. Meanwhile, Joe Ann bought inexpensive plastic curtains and set about making the little apartment an attractive place to live.

Like many young couples, the Ballards started their marriage on the brink of poverty. But even before the wedding, they had settled some of the big issues that often cause problems for a young couple. Joe Ann changed her membership to Monroe's church, because they felt husband and wife should worship together. The couple also agreed that they would handle financial matters through a joint account, and that they would pool their income to operate the household. In financial matters as in all their life together, there would be no such thing as "his" and "hers."

This kind of planning helped them avoid major difficulties. But there were still the trivial adjustments that all newlyweds face.

Joe Ann almost felt like screaming many times because Monroe was so detail-oriented; he gave copious explanations for everything. And he tired quickly of her incessant window shopping. Joe Ann had to get used to listening to her new husband's advice on ironing, cooking, and cleaning. And she had to learn that he wasn't the type to shower her with candy and gifts. He showed his affection in other ways.

"He may not bring me a dozen red roses," she told her sister-in-law, "but he sees that I have everything I need. I guess I just have to accept him the way he is."

As time passed, the seeds for their life's work were planted. As they successfully dealt with the little adjustments that every marriage brings, they were soon able to concentrate on the difficulties of others. Yet their work began so slowly and subtly that they hardly realized that they were beginning to build a unique ministry.

Driving through an impoverished neighborhood one day, they spotted a little boy playing by the road. He was wearing a dirty white T-shirt that came down to his knees, and his sneakers had holes in them.

"Sure wish we could get some clothes for that boy," Monroe sighed. "Someone needs to dress him a little better than that."

"Looks like he needs some food too," Joe Ann glanced back as they passed by. "He's all skin and bones."

While shopping, they watched a woman with dark circles under her eyes pulling a four-year-old child by the arm. Every few steps she slapped the crying child or pulled his hair.

The Ballards looked at each other and shook their heads sadly. They were thinking the same thing, but Monroe said it first. "No child deserves that kind of treatment. There's nothing wrong with spanking a kid if he's done wrong, but that mindless slapping and pulling doesn't accomplish a thing."

Joe Ann nodded. "Wish there was someone who

could help children like that."

As the young couple discussed these troubled children and the adults who showed so little concern, they grew increasingly disturbed. It wasn't just the poverty. Both of them were acquainted with poverty. It was the way these children were living—with no standards, no values, no discipline, no hope for anything better.

Monroe was especially disturbed because he encountered these problems every day in his sixth-grade class. So few of the children had fathers living at home. Most of them didn't have decent clothes. Nearly every child lacked confidence in himself.

One evening, several months after the birth of their first child, he came home in a grim mood.

"Did I ever tell you about Laura?" he asked Joe Ann, who was feeding baby Ephie on her lap. "She really bothers me. She's so lively, obedient, and willing to please. But I can't help feeling she's being defeated by the conditions of her home.

"You should see the dresses she wears to school, Joe Ann. They're practically threadbare, and they don't fit. She wears these awful boots, and she's obviously hungry. There I am giving out assignments, and I know she needs more help that I can possibly give from behind a desk."

Joe Ann thought for a moment. "Maybe we could find something else for her to wear."

Monroe, sitting at the dinner table with his head cradled in his hands, looked up suddenly. "Well, I don't see anything wrong with that, if you're willing."

"Why don't we invite her to our house for the weekend. We'll take her shopping and buy her some decent clothes."

The next day, Monroe talked to the girl's mother. She was thrilled that someone wanted to help the child, since she had eight other children to feed and clothe.

Nine-year-old Laura went home with Monroe from school the next Friday, and the Ballards' weekend program for children had begun. They took her shopping, carried her to church on Sunday, and taught her how to fly a homemade kite.

After Laura's visits, word of the Ballards' kindness spread throughout the neighborhood. Other young people from school and church started dropping in.

One Sunday Monroe and Joe Ann noticed two poorly dressed girls who were attending church with an old man. One looked as if she had never had a bath. Her clothes were worn and filthy. In fact, many of the members of the congregation resented her presence in their clean church.

But Joe Ann and Monroe had a more constructive reaction. They asked the girl's mother if she could come visit them on the weekend.

Monroe picked her up the following Saturday. She lived in a dilapidated shack with a front door that was barely hanging on its hinges. On the way to the Ballards' house in North Memphis, the youngster was quiet and reserved. But by the end of the day she was chattering as if she had known them forever.

"Lookit, Mr. Ballard. Lookit how Joe Ann washed my hair," she cried, running up to him Saturday afternoon.

The little girl had spent the morning getting to know Joe Ann. Like most children, she seemed comfortable calling her by her first name. After the shampoo, Joe Ann combed her hair and tied it with a bow. Then she took her to a department store and bought her a bright red dress, white stockings, and new Mary Jane shoes. That evening they could hardly tear the child away from the mirror for dinner.

The next day, the Ballards walked proudly into church with the little girl.

"Oooh, what a lovely child," cooed a woman with a fur coat and fancy hat.

Another woman stroked the girl's long curls. "Why, you're just a little doll, honey."

The Ballards were soon surrounded by church members who wanted to know all about this adorable child. They were shocked when they discovered she was the urchin who had repelled them only the Sunday before.

The couple's enthusiasm for giving practical help was not shared by many people in this congregation. Though they congratulated the Ballards on the transformation that had occurred in the little girl, when other dirty, smelly children turned up with the Ballards, the complaints started all over again.

"I can't go to a church that won't accept neglected children," Monroe lamented one Sunday evening. "Most of these people had rather throw a dirty child out then do something to change his condition."

Soon afterward the Ballards moved their church membership. At Friendship Church of the Nazarene, they renewed their efforts by filling their Sunday School classes with poor children from the surrounding community. After church, they usually took a group of about twenty of the young people home to dinner. Then they found out what the children needed most and tried to help them—first, by buying things with their own money and, later, by asking store owners for donations. They discovered that other people were eager to help, but often didn't know how to go about it.

A survey of department stores yielded treasure troves of slightly damaged items that would otherwise wind up on the junk heap. Most store managers were glad to save these items and contribute them to a good cause. Smaller neighborhood stores also gave them needed merchandise. Soon business firms all over the city began to think of the Ballards when they had articles to spare.

And when they had problems or needed help, the poor people of the community thought of the Ballards too.

*The Ballards showed me that the
Christian life doesn't have to be
dull or legalistic. Their home was
kind of a haven, I guess.*

—GLADYS GENERETTE
Missionary student

7

ENOUGH TO GO AROUND

You don't need a house number to find Joe Ann
and Monroe's place. If you know the street, you'll spot
it immediately. It's the modest, red brick house with the
motor home in front, a homemade merry-go-round in
back; a garage filled with broken-down appliances,
lumber, and tools; and a front porch covered with
boxes of donated clothing, shoes, and toys.

If you want to make sure it's the right place, just ask
the children. The little ones—well-dressed, polite, and
initially shy—are the Ballards' own children. Ephie, the
oldest, might be singing a gospel song or playing on a
home-made seesaw with her sister Linda, as their little
brother, Monroe Jr., watches from the swing set.

Or you might find Eric Wells, sixteen, working on a
bookshelf with two teenage girls. Tom, a white youth,
might be carrying a basketball hoop that Monroe has
repaired, while fifteen-year-old Marvin barbecues
chicken at the grill.

There's sure to be more activity inside the house—
watching the television or talking in the den; cooking in
the kitchen; playing in the living room. If you happen
to drop by on Saturday—some of the girls might be
sleeping late in the attic bedrooms, while downstairs
Wanda, who is going through a difficult stage, listens to
hygiene tips from Joe Ann. Nearby, two younger teenage girls help Ora Mae Benjamin, Joe Ann's foster
mother, by setting the two dining room tables for dinner.

These children know that the Ballard home is always open to them. Joe Ann and Monroe try to provide whatever is needed—a haven from a chaotic world for one child; a model for Christian living for another; guidance for repairing a bicycle for a third.

Every one of these young people—and over 250 others to whom the Ballards have ministered since 1966—have their own reasons for visiting this home. Each person could tell his own heart-wrenching story . . .

• Gladys Generette, a young missionary student, was reared by caring parents with strong religious beliefs. Fascinated by the occult, attracted to the violent doctrine of the Black Panthers, she began to shut out her parents and her faith. "I always believed in God, but I didn't want Him to have anything to do with my life," she recalled. "I grew unstable in my Christian life and rebellious at home."

Frantic with worry, her mother lost control. She demanded that her daughter get home at a decent hour and stay off the streets at night. "She resented anything I asked her to do," Bertha Generette later remembered. "My greatest fear was that in her rebellion against us she would fall in with the wrong crowd."

Luckily Gladys found the *right* crowd. Her family had known the Ballards through their church for several years. Joe Ann and Monroe had asked her to visit many times. She remembered those invitations during a time of crisis. Confused, torn between two worlds, she started dropping in for weekends at the red brick house. She was ready, in many ways, to return to the values of her Christian home, but she was trapped in her own rebellion. Joe Ann and Monroe's open house gave her the boost she needed to find her way back.

Gladys remembers picnics, talks, and meals with the Ballard family—simple activities that touched her with a profound message. "The Ballards showed me that the Christian life doesn't have to be dull or legalistic. They did mostly fun things. This gave me and other young people a positive attitude toward Christianity."

• Tom is a soft-spoken teenager with shaggy blond hair and more than his share of family problems. His two teenage sisters dropped out of high school when they had babies before they were fifteen. His mother and stepfather have a stormy, on-again, off-again marriage, complicated by his inability to get along with the children. Time after time, Tom's mother would leave her husband, but she would come back "as sure as the sun rises every day," according to Joe Ann.

In that confusing environment, Tom grew into his teen years with a mind of his own. As time passed, he found it difficult to maintain a truce with his stepfather while his mother was sorting out her life. The Ballards' "home away from home" was just what he needed to escape these family problems for a while. With his mother's consent, he moved into their motor home for a month. This helped him avoid more restrictive institutional aid.

"We realized that if he went to juvenile court or the welfare department, they might put him in a state- supported foster home," explained Joe Ann. "Since he was almost eighteen, he was too old for that. We know that Tom is able to handle his own business, but what agency would know that?"

Had Tom had been forced to take the route that led to reports, red tape, and heavy social worker caseloads, he might still be in a foster home.

• Sixteen-year-old Eric Wells, who assists the pastor at Memphis South Church of the Nazarene, is known as "Rev" to many of his fellow tenth-graders. They seek him out for advice. Slim and handsome, he flashes an easy smile and projects a warm, outgoing manner.

In the Ballards' home, Eric has become an example to other young people. When advice is given, he's the first to listen. When someone needs help, he's ready to lend a hand. But he hasn't always been like this. At thirteen, when he first came to Memphis South, he was lazy and apathetic. "He wouldn't think of doing anything on his own," Joe Ann emphasized. "We've seen a drastic change in him."

Becoming a Christian made a dramatic difference in Eric's life. Before he was converted, he lived like most of his classmates and neighbors—experimenting with cigarettes and alcohol, imitating those around him.

Joe Ann and Monroe worked with Eric, but so did other concerned Christians. Their pastor and other church members also took an interest in the likable teenager. The big change in his life grew out of a spiritual awareness that was carefully cultivated. From Joe Ann and Monroe he received clothes, food, and attention. From their consistent example he learned about the benefits of hard work and persistence. "Monroe is always saying, 'Don't give up. Do your best,' " Eric said. Monroe's motto is: 'Through God, all things are possible.' I think it's good to have a saying you can live by. That's mine too."

Eric has no father at home, so he has accepted Monroe as a combination father-brother. The Ballards have projected a clear picture of what a father should do and how a family should act together.

"Eric is almost grown, but he respects me like a little

child," Monroe told a recent visitor. "If I tell him something he needs to know, he listens. If he needs a little something and doesn't have the money, he doesn't mind asking. It's the sort of thing that he missed out on when he was growing up without a father."

When Eric first began visiting with the Ballards, it was the little things that surprised him. "I'll always remember them sitting around the dinner table *together*, talking to each other about what happened during the week. In most large families, one person eats and then another person eats. They don't sit down together."

Their experience with Eric has been particularly satisfying to Joe Ann and Monroe because so many people have noticed the improvement in his attitude. "We don't see such a drastic change in every child," Joe Ann admitted, "but it's gratifying to work with one like Eric. He represents the children who might have fallen by the wayside."

• When Adrienne, fourteen, ran away from home, her grandmother made two phone calls—one to the police and the other to the Ballards. She explained that the girl had emerged from her apathetic, trance-like behavior into a state of outright rebellion. She sounded so frantic that the Ballards went to her house to talk to her.

"While we were talking with the grandmother, Adrienne walked in," Monroe explained. "She seemed to be in a stupor and I asked her to sit down. Joe Ann and I kept talking, afraid she might get up and leave at any minute. But she sat still and listened. In a little while, she started crying. But she kept insisting that she planned to run away from home again.

"Suddenly I leaped forward in my seat, tears in my

eyes. 'Go ahead and give your grandmother a hard time,' I dared her. 'Live with your friends. Get into trouble. But remember that even then—we will help you. We will find you and we'll help you.'

"We left shortly after that, not knowing if we had helped or hurt the situation. When Joe Ann called later, she discovered that Adrienne had left again and returned. She had decided to stay with her grandmother and try to stay out of trouble."

The Ballards sent her a watch for Christmas. The unsigned card simply read: *Merry Christmas, Adrienne.*

• The Williams family had been causing quite a commotion at church. Their four unmanageable little boys were almost tearing the place up. The young mother, a high school dropout, had no control. She didn't seem to know what to do. Although she had four children, she was scarcely more than a child herself.

Over a period of time, Joe Ann and Monroe began to encourage her. "You're smart," Joe Ann told her. "Why don't you try getting your high school equivalency diploma?" Mrs. Williams eventually did just that and found a job. Meanwhile, the children stayed with the Ballards.

Joe Ann and Monroe provided some of the order that had been missing. "They learned just by observing us," Joe Ann explained. "We spent a lot of time with the mother. By watching me around the house, she learned how to keep her kids clean."

The boys also improved in their behavior after being around the Ballard family. No one had ever shown them how to act. But they soon discovered at the Ballards that good behavior is a lot more fun than bad behavior.

The Ballards' ministry touches many children other than those who live with them or visit them on weekends. For some youngsters, their first experience in eating out comes when the Ballards take them to a local cafeteria. And Joe Ann has developed connections with many Memphis stores. This means that hundreds of children receive shirts, pants, shoes, watches, dresses, and toys that their own parents can't afford.

One Easter, Joe Ann learned that a department store had overstocked on chocolate Easter bunnies. She loaded 1,500 into her car, and, with Monroe's help, distributed them in housing projects and other poor neighborhoods.

Providing a happier Christmas for children is another Ballard project. Several years ago, Joe Ann came up with the idea of a community Christmas party. She told a newspaper reporter that she would provide Christmas dinner for two hundred children, even if it meant feeding them tuna fish sandwiches.

When people read her statement in the paper, they quickly responded. With some donations, supplemented by their own money, the Ballards bought 250 presents. They hired a restaurant to cater the affair in their own home. About 225 children showed up!

It took Monroe and Joe Ann two weeks to recuperate from that first event. But they have continued it every year since, with increasing help from the community. One year a wealthy citizen of Memphis donated $2,000 for the Christmas gifts. It looks as if that has also become an annual tradition.

"Things like this happen all the time," Joe Ann said. "Somehow, a person's heart moves over to the right place at the right time."

Because Joe Ann and Monroe are
willing to live what they teach,
people believe what they say.

REV. SYLVESTER BALLARD

8

PRACTICING WHAT YOU PREACH

One day Monroe was picking his way through an automobile junkyard with a preacher friend. Aggressive and young, the preacher was a real fire-and-brimstone man—someone who could stir you right out of your seat with his sermons.

After picking out an ignition part for his car, the preacher came upon a brake cable he needed. While Monroe watched, he picked it up and put it in his pocket. "I think I can sneak this out without paying for it," he told the dumbfounded teacher. Then he walked into the junk dealer's office, paid for the ignition part only, and left.

"That really bothers me," Monroe told his wife later. "He's supposed to be an upright, Christian man. How could he take something without paying for it?"

Joe Ann was just as horrified. She had watched other adults rationalize cases of petty theft. A maid pockets the nickels and dimes on her employer's dresser because she feels underpaid. A shopper doesn't point out a cashier's undercharging error, feeling "prices are too high anyway." Joe Ann knew from experience that these same people probably tell their youngsters that it's wrong to steal.

After twelve years of helping young people, the Ballards have developed some firm ideas about child rearing. Their guiding principle is that children need good examples, not just good words. If a parent lectures on the evils of liquor while tipping his bottle, his children won't believe him. According to Joe Ann, the most traumatic experience for a child is to discover that his parents are phonies. "Many kids hear their parents talk about religion, but then the parents live like the devil," she said. "How can children understand this kind of religion? They grow up thinking the adult world is a hoax."

When children come to visit them, Joe Ann and Monroe make sure they don't display this kind of hypocrisy. Their rules are simple and firm: No smoking, drinking, or profanity is allowed. Girls and women wear dresses. Children must treat their elders with respect. The teenagers who live with them must tell them where they are going before they leave the house, and are expected home at a reasonable hour. Some kids resent these restrictions, but Joe Ann believes they are necessary. They tell the kids very clearly where the Ballards stand.

Joe Ann and Monroe have also developed a strict code of ethics for their work. They accept no donations of money for their ministry, unless it's earmarked for a specific purpose, such as the Christmas party. And they won't sell the merchandise donated by stores. They scrupulously avoid any hint of dishonesty. "Some stores even encourage us to sell the merchandise they donate," Monroe explained. "But money is dangerous because it can be used in so many different ways. Clothes and other items can only be used as they're made."

Although the Ballards are people of simple tastes, some of their self-imposed regulations do take discipline. Joe Ann admits that a load of merchandise sometimes contains items she would like to have. But to compromise her principles would be dishonest and disastrous. "Sometimes we get some beautiful dresses. But I realize that Mary Jane or some other person needs them more than I do. It's a matter of discipline.

In this kind of ministry, you have to keep your own desires under control."

Their rules have often led them to refuse gifts that others would jump at. One man read about their work and offered to buy them a $10,000 motor home. But Monroe felt they had no use for it. "We aren't dealing with things for things' sake," he explained. "We are working toward specific objectives. What would we do with a $10,000 trailer that we couldn't use?"

Joe Ann and Monroe are just as responsible in the management of their own household. Instead of buying and spending on impulse, they budget carefully to pay their own expenses and help others. Their combined $30,000 salary stretches so far that neighbors, friends, and relatives can't believe it. "Some people must think we have a money tree that we shake every few days," Joe Ann laughed. "They don't know how hard we work to make ends meet."

Here, in their own words, are some other important principles that Monroe and Joe Ann communicate to the children who live and visit in their home.

Cleanliness—The Bible talks about people with "clean hands and a pure heart" (Ps. 24:4). We believe cleanliness around a house is essential. We teach the children how to handle dishes, and how to wash them. Some of these children have never used soap before. They have been accustomed to rinsing the dishes under the faucet.

We also teach the children how to change the sheets on their beds. We don't let them skip two or three weeks. We encourage them to do it every Friday or Saturday, and even more often than that if necessary.

Some parents don't think about these things, or they can't provide extra clothes for the kids to change into or money for the laundry. They know little about home sanitation. We make sure these kids learn some health rules.

Sharing—We started teaching children to share at an early age. When he was only a year old, Monroe Jr. would say, "Mama, I'm going to share with Linda." If a child learns to share his toys, he can apply that principle to more important things later in life.

Many of the children who visit us live in homes where candy is hidden and the refrigerator is guarded. Their parents won't share, so the children learn to steal. If a mother hides a candy bar in her dresser, the children will be tempted to sneak in to get it. At our house we make treats like this available to everyone.

We can't afford expensive foods, but we can buy a box of bruised cantaloupes, cut out the bad parts, and have enough for everyone. Instead of expensive cuts of beef, we buy enough chicken to guarantee second helpings.

Sometimes this is a real shock to the kids. If they sneak an apple from the kitchen, we tell them they're welcome to that apple. They can have whatever they want as long as they don't waste. When we share with them, they realize they can share too.

Avoiding Waste—Many adults have a bad habit of throwing usable things out. If their television breaks, they go in debt to buy a new one. Or they buy a new car when they could have gotten some more mileage from the old one. Once we found a lamp in the garbage where one of our foster daughters had thrown it. The on-off switch had gone bad. We explained that the switch was easy to repair. But even if something more serious were wrong, the lamp had several parts that could be salvaged and recycled. We tried to teach her a lesson in thrift and conservation.

People waste too much these days. We'll go to a rundown shack where the men are unemployed and find them throwing away clothes or furniture that could be used. Or a child will pour the orange juice she didn't drink down the drain. Or a mother will let some food turn bad when her family really needed it. Poverty feeds on wasteful attitudes like these.

At our house we don't throw out broken machines — we fix them. We don't discard good clothes just because they're out of fashion — we find someone who needs them. We don't pour out half a glass of orange juice — we take only what we can drink. It's amazing how much you can save if you cut down on needless waste.

Saving — We don't tell the children they need bank accounts. But we talk about how important it is to save money for the future. If our utility bill is lower than normal one month, we might use that extra cash to pay the car insurance, or we might put it in the bank. We don't spend it foolishly just because we have a little extra. These young people notice our example. It teaches them to save too.

Confidence — So many of the children we help lack confidence. We keep encouraging them to try. We tell them they have no reason to fail unless they sit around doing nothing.

We want them to set goals and work at them. We encourage them to begin thinking now about some things they would like to do someday. Then they won't have to think about this decision after they are on their own.

Listening and Learning — Some people think they're too old to learn. People make too much of their age. We try not to do that at our house. Sometimes we treat all these kids like little children because they missed some important rules of behavior or health when they were growing up.

They don't resent it because we make it into a little game. We'll ask them, "Did you little children wash your hands?" They usually get the message without taking offense.

Responsibility—We show kids that we're responsible for our actions. We back up what we say by keeping our promises. Some kids don't trust anyone because they have been let down by so many people. We show them the importance of following through.

There are some days we don't feel like getting up early and going to work or picking up a load of clothes. But we do it because it's our duty. This teaches the kids not to let down on *their* responsibility.

After many years in this ministry, Monroe and Joe Ann have learned some important principles of working with children.

First, every child is treated as an individual. "Children are different," Joe Ann emphasizes. "You have to deal with each one at his level of understanding." A child is who is wild and rebellious might need firm discipline and strong words, while a shy, sensitive child would respond to a quiet explanation of his mistake. The Ballards might recommend college for one high school senior, trade school for another. They avoid the temptation to compare children and press them into molds.

Consistency is another important principle in their work with children. A parent shouldn't reprimand a youngster for talking in church one day, they point out, then ignore him when he does it again. "Some parents fuss at a child for something he does and warn him not to do it again," Monroe said, shaking his head. "But they don't follow up to make sure the child obeys. This creates a kind of disorder in his life. Soon he reaches the point where he will do anything. You have to be consistent in your demands for good behavior. If you let little problems slide by with no discipline, you'll soon be faced with big ones."

Another secret of this couple's successful work with children is persistence. Even when they seem to be dealing with a hopeless case, they remind themselves that no child is impossible. After years of experience, they find it easier now to keep trying. They can remember the people who practically laughed at the idea of Karice and Anna going to college, or the social worker who labeled Alison a "poor investment."

"We've worked with many children who were supposed to be incorrigible," Joe Ann says. "Sometimes, when we've done our best, a child does something that is totally foreign to our way of life. That's discouraging. But we keep trying. We have to stick by him. Wouldn't it be tragic to give up on a child just as he is about to reach the turning point?"

*Suppose there are brothers or sisters who
need clothes and don't have enough to
eat. What good is there in your saying to
them, "God bless you! Keep warm and eat
well!"—if you don't give them the
necessities of life?*

JAMES 2:15-16, TEV

9

GIVING ISN'T EASY

Monroe and Joe Ann make giving look so easy.
Could other people succeed at the same kind of
ministry?

Not only do the Ballards believe it is possible, but
they hope people all over the country will realize that
giving to others is a responsibility. But they are also
aware of the pitfalls and difficulties that a family faces
when they open their door to strangers. Will people
take advantage of you? Sure. Will they smother you
with gratitude? Probably not. To do this kind of work, a
person has to be prepared for problems. His motives
for serving others must be right. He has to be strong
enough to serve as a support for others.

Over the years, several friends, relatives, and acquaintances have tried to copy the Ballards' work.
Some have been successful. Others, without stability or
deep commitment, have failed. Here are their stories,
in fictionalized form, with Joe Ann and Monroe's
analysis of each situation.

Doris and Frank Green have known the Ballards for
some time. Frank, a teacher friend of Monroe's, is an
intense person with gray eyes and expressive
eyebrows. His wife, Doris, is a petite young woman ten
years younger.

She dropped out of college when they married and

devoted her energies to being a full-time wife. She doted on Frank, making his favorite dishes for dinner and running endless errands for him. Once his idle comment about a movie star's hair style sent her dashing to the beauty parlor for a similar cut.

Frank was so impressed by the Ballards' work that he had planned to follow their example after his marriage. He and his wife celebrated their first wedding anniversary by applying to become foster parents. Within a month, a fifteen-year-old girl was placed in their home.

Doris had agreed to the arrangement, but secretly she was not too enthusiastic about it. Faced with a rebellious teenager so soon after her own adolescence, she quickly lost all interest in the project. Days after the girl's arrival, she discovered that Sandy was more interested in developing a good relationship with her husband than with her.

All day long Doris and Sandy argued. "You can't tell me to make my bed. I won't do it," the teenager whined. "You're not my mother, so don't boss me around."

When Frank got home at night, Sandy's disobedient, nasty streak vanished. "Why can't you two get along?" he asked after hearing Sandy's complaints and seeing his wife's agitation. "The poor girl has been through enough, Doris. Can't you treat her with kindness?"

As the weeks passed, Sandy grew to trust Frank more and more. The two talked late into the night about the girl's many problems. For the first time in her life, she began to feel that someone understood her. But Doris was about to explode. Upset by her own failure to communicate with Sandy and distraught over the loss of Frank's attention, she began to imagine a possible romantic attraction between the two.

The situation got so bad that Frank finally had to let Sandy find another foster home. The tragedy was that she seemed to be making progress. He had been able to break her pattern of rudeness and disrespect to adults that had developed over the years. She had started to talk about her future instead of bewailing her lousy childhood. But that progress stopped when she was removed from the Greens' home. To Sandy, this was just one more injustice in a long string of injustices. The experience turned out badly for everyone concerned.

The Ballards Comment: It is futile for a husband and wife to become involved in something like this unless both are equally committed. Doris went along with the project just to please her husband. She lacked the security and experience to be a foster parent. We weren't much older than she when we started, but both of us were committed to the activity, and we were secure in our own relationship. If you're dealing with teenagers, you have to be a mature adult yourself.

Don and Gloria Seeker had a different problem. They wanted to do nice things for people, but they wanted to make sure that everyone knew about their good deeds. They dreamed about being recognized as upstanding members of the community—people who were sought out for advice and assistance.

Not wanting to be outdone in good works by Joe Ann and Monroe, they started inviting children to their house. They even went after some of the young people who were already coming to the Ballards. For about a month three teenage girls dropped out of Joe Ann and Monroe's Saturday activities. When Gloria and Don tired of them, they came back.

Actually, the Seekers were not overly fond of

children anyway. But they did try. The first weekend Gloria made a big dinner for the girls, and the group spent the afternoon playing ball together. When the girls showed little enthusiasm, the Seekers were disappointed.

The couple didn't know what to do with their guests the next weekend. Gloria finally took the girls shopping. The young people wandered off by themselves, and everyone got upset when Gloria complained. At dinner fourteen-year-old Patricia's behavior was particularly galling. She rejected the blackberry pie for dessert and refused to talk to the others.

"Why should I spend all day in the kitchen, making dinner for these kids, when they don't even appreciate it," Gloria screamed at Don that evening after he had taken the girls back home. "Not a single one thanked us for what we did today."

The next Saturday Gloria stayed in bed because she felt sick. Don gave the kids peanut butter and jelly sandwiches. Don spent the following weekend repairing his car, while Gloria and the girls watched an old movie on television. Finally Gloria played sick again and the Seekers' weekend program fizzled out.

The Ballards Comment: Gloria and Don were looking for reinforcement from the children for what they were doing. You can't expect children to thank you all the time. Besides, you ought to help people because they need it, not because they appreciate it. The Seekers were more concerned with results than with the effort. In this ministry, helping children has to serve as its own reward.

We spent a lot of money and time before anyone knew what we were doing. Knowing that you're doing what's right should be satisfaction enough.

In a more affluent black neighborhood in Memphis live two other acquaintances of the Ballards, *John and Sharon Bounty*. He is a successful young lawyer and college professor and drives a sports car. They live in a large, modern house. Sharon wears expensive jewelry and the latest fashions.

While they don't mind spending money on themselves, they are also concerned about their less fortunate "poor black brothers." About once a month Sharon gathers discarded clothes to take to the rundown Memphis community where some of her relatives still live.

"Things are going so well for us, we wanted you to have these," she once told a former neighbor. "We know you and your poor little children can always use something extra."

Several times, after a condescending speech, Sharon was shocked when her friends refused to accept her clothes. They let her know they didn't want her coming around with her designer dresses and expensive jewelry. Sharon met Joe Ann at a store one day and told her about the frustrating end to her philanthropic work. "Let us try giving the clothes to your old neighbors," Joe Ann suggested gently. The Bounty family agreed. And the people who had turned Sharon away accepted the clothes from the Ballards.

The Ballards Comment: Sharon and John apparently had an air of "handing down" to the people. This just won't work.

We identify with poor people. We know how they live. We're not in the Cadillac bracket, so it's easy for us to relate to the poor and for them to relate to us. We try to give them the feeling that we're sharing with them because they are our friends. We don't give them the impression that we're so rich we can afford to give food and clothes away. Whether or not they meant to, that's the impression Sharon and John gave.

Willie and Goldie Digger assisted the Ballards for a while with store pickups. Goldie called the stores and drove her station wagon to pick up items. The process went smoothly, except for one thing.

Their own children, neighbors, and relatives went through the boxes to pick out the good merchandise for themselves. A new watch went on the wrist of the Diggers' ten-year-old son, Tony. A pair of men's running shoes found their way to Willie's feet. By the time the Diggers hauled the merchandise to a community center, it looked like the leftovers from a rummage sale. After several experiences like that, Joe Ann and Monroe resumed the pickups themselves.

The Ballards Comment: When a merchant donates something for your ministry, you can't keep the best for yourself. These items should go to the people who need them. This is the only way you can continue to operate with integrity. You shouldn't benefit materially yourself as Willie and Goldie tried to do. This is just another form of stealing.

We know that in all things God works for good with those who love him, those whom he has called according to his purpose.

ROMANS 8:28, TEV

10

TAKING ADVANTAGE OF DISADVANTAGES

The sad experiences of the Diggers and the Seekers show what can happen when couples do "good works" for personal gain or praise. And the Bountys and the Greens are proof that a person can't give successfully to others without the right attitude. Also essential is a stable and secure personality.

But even when a person's motives are right, plenty can go wrong. Joe Ann and Monroe know. They've had their share of problems. Miscarriages and a traumatic car accident have sapped Joe Ann's energy. Financial emergencies have put the couple in debt. Relatives have sometimes resented their work. Some people have even tried to take advantage of their kindness.

In order to survive these ups and downs, they point out, a person needs to take advantage of his disadvantages. "We try to learn from our problems," Joe Ann insists. "One good thing about difficulties is that they help you identify with people. You just can't let problems get you down. You have to learn from them and then go on."

As an example, she cites the automobile accident she had several years ago. A plumbing truck smashed into her car when she ran a stop sign. Neither driver was injured, but Joe Ann was deeply shaken and overcome with guilt when she looked at their vehicles and all the debris from the crash. *Someone could have been killed by my carelessness,* she thought.

87

Although she tried to keep her fears and shame hidden, they nearly incapacitated her during the next few months. Sometimes, just thinking about driving caused her to tremble violently. "If I had something important to do, my uncontrollable shakiness got worse," she recalls. "If I had to drive somewhere, I would think about it all day, with growing dread."

While experiencing these fears, Joe Ann had a tubal pregnancy that further complicated her emotional strain and confusion. "I had trouble distinguishing between my physical problems and my mental ones," Joe Ann recalled. "I thought I might be going crazy. I had to force myself to go to work, to care for my family, and to be friendly to people."

But the young mother also summoned the will to pray and read the scriptures every night. Gradually the situation improved. "I could feel myself being delivered from the guilt and fear. I never would have chosen to go through that experience deliberately. But I look at it now as a lesson that helps me better understand people with emotional problems."

Later she met a woman whose son had been struck down by a car. Although the boy wasn't killed, he was severely injured, and his mother insisted that the accident was her fault—that she hadn't watched her son closely enough. Joe Ann talked with her for hours. By describing her own accident and the relief she had found in prayer, she helped the woman work through her guilt feelings.

Another time, Joe Ann received a desperate telephone call from the former girlfriend of her brother-in-law. On the brink of suicide, she was reaching out to the Ballards in a last-minute plea for help. Joe Ann talked to her for three hours until she promised not to hurt herself. "I told her what had happened to me. I couldn't have related to her unless I had experienced similar feelings myself. I had never thought about suicide, but there were times in my experience when I wondered if death might be a comfort. I assured her that all of us have our weak moments, but we can't let ourselves give in to them. She listened."

At other times, Joe Ann and Monroe have come perilously close to financial disaster. They recall one particular series of emergencies that put them in the hole. Joe Ann was hospitalized twice because of miscarriages. While arranging Alison's wedding, they were still paying for her trip from Colorado to Memphis the year before. On top of that, they refused to give up the annual Christmas party, which usually costs them about $300. To meet all their expenses, they had to borrow $2,500.

This experience taught them to budget and plan for emergencies. Now they have better insurance, a travel fund, a Christmas fund, and a larger savings reserve. By tighter budgeting, they have cut down on wasteful, needless spending. By managing through the difficulties without skimping on their projects, they have come through with increased confidence.

They have developed this same positive attitude toward many other hardships. Monroe frequently tells about his early troubles in school in order to motivate other poor students. Joe Ann's abandonment by her natural mother gives her a better understanding of all abandoned children. His poverty as a child helps him relate to poor people. Her difficulty in finding a job when she first came to Memphis makes Joe Ann sympathetic toward the unemployed and a ready resource to help others find work.

The Ballards feel that people can grow stronger if

they will face up to their problems and not give up. "None of us has been promised a lazy, trouble-free life," Monroe says. "As long as you're alive you may struggle. And the struggle builds character and determination."

Petty annoyances accompany the Ballards' work. Like all human beings, they are sometimes bothered by the quirks and habits of other people. Since they are surrounded by others most of the time, they have to work harder than most to control their irritation.

Since the second year of their marriage, they have housed other people in their home. First, Joe Ann's mother came to live with them; then, Monroe's brothers, Sam and Sylvester; next, a cousin; then a woman with three children who needed a temporary home; and, finally, the Ballards' four foster daughters.

It took time for the Ballard family to learn to accept the irritating habits of others. At first Joe Ann was annoyed by rings in the bathtub, slamming doors, and footsteps that thumped at all hours on the attic floor. But she finally realized that such little things were only a temporary nuisance. She adjusted to them. Now she and Monroe try to ignore the bothersome habits of others. They comment on certain disturbing practices—like smacking at the table or being messy— only if they seem to be detrimental to the people who practice them.

And then there are those people who take advantage of their generosity. One youth, for example, kept coming to them for bus fare to get to his job. They knew he earned enough money to pay for his own transportation. But they gave him bus fare anyway, with the understanding that this borrowing would stop when his salary checks started coming regularly. Their patience kept him on the job and eventually ended his dependency.

Instead of confronting a youngster about things like this, their normal policy is to keep giving to him. They have discovered that a person eventually stops asking for help which he doesn't need. "Sure, kids take advantage of you, but all people do that to a certain degree," Joe Ann insists. "This shouldn't prevent us as Christians from reaching out to help."

Adults try their patience too. The Ballards have learned to say no in some of these situations. Joe Ann has to make it clear to some mothers that her house is not available as a free babysitting service. When a person asks for cash, the Ballards usually refuse because of a bad experience they had several years ago.

A man asked for a loan to pay a furniture bill. Monroe withdrew the money from his credit union account and loaned it to the man, but he skipped town and never repaid the loan. Now they realize there are times when you have to draw the line for a person's own good.

The reaction of some friends to their "foster" daughters has presented another problem for the Ballards. The young women aren't welcomed in these homes as openly as the Ballards' own children.

Another uncomfortable situation developed when Joe Ann and Monroe went away for the weekend and left Karice and Anna in charge of the house. A friend came by to borrow the car. But Karice wouldn't let him have it because Joe Ann hadn't left word that it was all right. The man was furious. "Those girls don't belong here anyway," he told the couple later. "They're trying to take over."

The Ballards accepted the outburst calmly. They

believed Karice had done the right thing, and they told her so. Not even the opinions of well-meaning friends can stop them from doing what they think is right.

Monroe and Joe Ann realize that their open house makes them vulnerable to criticism and gossip, but they don't worry about it. "We don't feel a need to defend ourselves," Monroe said. "If somebody claims we're nothing but fakes, we don't waste our time arguing with him. We just keep on doing our work. We let our critics know that we would help them, too, if they got into trouble.

"We don't receive any grants from agencies. We support this ministry with our own money. This brings authority and integrity to our work. It's hard to think ill of a person for very long when you see him giving of himself and his earthly goods to help others."

Joe Ann and Monroe are a refreshing contrast to the packaged caring services offered by government agencies. They are living proof that individuals who care about others really can make a difference. Opening their hearts to others has not sapped their strength. Indeed, it seems to have made them stronger.

*Many people take a dim view of their
responsibility. But they forget that all
welfare and asistance used to come from
the church or individuals.*

MONROE BALLARD

11

PEOPLE HELPING PEOPLE

Memphis, Tennessee, typical of many large cities, has more than a thousand agencies, services, clubs and organizations that specialize in helping people. City, county, and state all have human service departments. Food stamps and authorizations-to-purchase cards are churned out each month. During the winter, the poor line up at the Community Action Agency to ask for help with their utility bills. The Boys' Clubs, Girls' Club, YMCA, YWCA, and a score of other agencies sponsor programs to keep young people off the streets. Family Service of Memphis and the mental health centers provide family and individual counseling. Some sixty organizations help senior citizens eat right, fill their leisure time, protect themselves against crime, and keep themselves healthy.

Foster care programs are sponsored by the Tennessee Department of Human Services, juvenile court, and several other agencies. The Urban League, NAACP, city Community Relations division, the Equal Employment Opportunity Commission, and the Congress of Racial Equality all work for racial justice. The Comprehensive Employment Training Act creates hundreds of jobs for the unemployed. The government provides financial aid to people over 65, poor mothers, the disabled, and those who have lost their jobs. Community groups provide food and clothes for the indigent. Public hospitals, nursing homes, and boarding houses provide a shelter of last resort. The list goes on and on.

In fact, it has become so long that many of these agencies are providing duplicate services. But most of them have little idea what the others provide. A person seeking help is frequently in the dark about where to turn. Many are bounced from one place to another in the game of "agency referral."

To Joe Ann, who has worked in several social service agencies, the game is familiar. "Many of them play 'pass the buck' very well. With so many services available, it's easy to send people who need help to another address."

The Ballards can recall many cases where these agencies haven't come through with needed assistance.

They remember one woman whose Social Security benefits were mysteriously cut off. After trying to explain the problem to the local Social Security office, she called the Ballards in frustration. Joe Ann dialed the office to see what she could find out.

"I'm sorry, ma'am, but we can't release that information to you," said a bored voice at the other end of the line.

"But I sent you a notarized letter from Mrs. Smith authorizing me to handle her business. It should be in the files," Joe Ann explained.

"The files are in another department. There's nothing we can do."

"May I talk to your supervisor?"

"He can't be reached at this number. He's on another line."

"May I have that number?"

"Sorry. I've been instructed not to release that information."

So the conversation went. When Joe Ann realized she wasn't getting anywhere, she hung up and called again—and again—and again. Finally, when it became clear that she wouldn't give up, she was transferred to a supervisor. After an apology, he settled the problem.

At Christmas one year a woman with a serious skin disease called the Ballards from her hospital bed. She had been trying to find someone who could help her buy Christmas presents for her eight children. Already she had talked to nine agencies. Since it was late in the season, none of them could provide clothes, food, or gifts for all the children. "We just don't have enough money in our budget right now," she was told.

The Ballards didn't have enough money in their budget, either, but they called several department stores and food markets. Within four hours, they had rounded up Christmas presents for all the children.

Many people call the Ballards when they see someone who needs counseling, clothes, food, shelter, or a job. Why don't these people give the aid themselves? They usually explain that they just don't have enough time.

One request for aid came from the office of a government official in Washington, D.C. A staff assistant called to ask whether the couple could provide food and diapers for the family of a man who had been accidentally shot. Joe Ann and Monroe put together a basket of food, bought the diapers, and headed for the house of this family whom they had never met. They were happy to help. But they were also disappointed that neither the official nor the aides in his office thought of offering the help themselves.

"It does seem strange, doesn't it?" Joe Ann puzzled, shaking her head. "They call us—two people with no resources other than our own—to take care of this need. Our two salaries are nowhere near what that man earns. I doubt if they would equal his expense money."

The Ballards realize that an elected government official has a constituency of thousands of poor people. He couldn't help them all with money from his own pocket. But they also believe that people, whatever their jobs, should recognize their individual responsibility to care for others. It isn't a new idea, of course, just one that has been lost somewhere along the way.

While preparing several bushels of fresh vegetables for the freezer one day, Joe Ann talked about how people used to help one another. "Things were different when I was a little girl. If a person in my hometown died and the family couldn't afford to bury him, the church and the town took on that responsibility. When the roof on our house was damaged, the neighbors helped my father fix it. And during his last illness, they took turns coming over to help my mother."

Joe Ann and Monroe have tried to transfer that tradition of neighborliness to Memphis. They don't oppose social service agencies. They often work with them to help people. But they realize that programmed aid has its limitations. They feel strongly that the most worthy organizations can't take the place of people helping other people.

They base that belief on the success of their own work—their ability to do what institutions often cannot do. They become friends with the people whom they help. This means they can respond to individual needs. Because they work with people in their home, they can show them how to lead more useful, efficient lives. *Showing* is better than *telling*. They hire no employees, so they avoid the hassle of supervision and employee dishonesty. With no red tape or restrictive regulations, they don't require "clients" to spend hours filling out forms. Since they feel they're "on call" as Christians at all times, they don't stop answering their phone nor do they lock their door at 5 p.m.

"An institution has to spend much of its time protecting itself," Monroe points out. "It has to worry about getting the next grant, making sure that no one is cheating, and developing good relationships with the people and organizations who support it. We don't have to protect ourselves like that because our organization is simple. We're the headquarters *and* the field representatives."

Unfortunately, the Ballards' work has one obvious limitation. Since their organization is simple and person-centered, they can help only a few people at one time. They can't minister to the masses. In a wishful tone, tinged with hope, they speak of an ideal world where every person recognizes his duty to others. This is the responsibility of all faiths, they believe, but it especially applies to Christians.

"The Bible instructs us to serve as our brother's keeper," Joe Ann says. "We're supposed to care for the poor, the widows, and the orphans. But in our denomination, at least in the black churches, there's probably no more than half a dozen people who are concerned about the physical needs as well as the spiritual needs of people. Many Christians think that if they just pray for a person, God will take care of his physical needs. But the Bible makes it plain that we should get involved in meeting those needs ourselves."

Joe Ann and Monroe cite many Bible passages to support their belief.

"There is more happiness in giving than in receiving" (Acts 20:35b, TEV).

"None of us lives for himself only" (Rom. 14:7a, TEV).

"When you give to the poor, it is like lending to the Lord" (Prov. 19:17a, TEV).

"Happy are those who are concerned for the poor" (Ps. 41:1a, TEV).

"Give to others, and God will give to you" (Luke 6:38a, TEV).

"Give to the poor and you will never be in need" (Prov. 28:27a, TEV).

Unfortunately, Monroe points out, many Christians seem to be neglecting their responsibility in this area. Joe Ann is quick to agree. "Too many Christians leave it to somebody else, who passes it on to another person. It's almost like an agency referral."

To prove their point, Joe Ann and Monroe recall the example of one church they belonged to for a while. The church did not permit them to use its building as a clothes distribution center. The pastor couldn't find authorization for the activity in his church manual.

Joe Ann and Monroe have also discovered that selfishness is a powerful force. Typically, a neighbor who learns about a bargain at a nearby store will keep the information secret. Another person who hears about a clothes giveaway will keep quiet so he can get the best clothes for himself and his family.

The Ballards have heard every selfish excuse in the book that people use to avoid becoming involved in a ministry to the poor:

"When I get off from work, I'm just too tired."

"I have my own family to take care of."

"I can't cook well enough."

"My house is too small."

"I don't have enough money."

But perhaps the biggest hindrance to helping is the feeling of many people that they can't really change things. Many are bogged down in the fatalistic belief that their efforts really wouldn't do any good. "Instead of getting up and carrying others with them, they just continue to walk on the ones who need help," Monroe sighs.

The Ballards would like to change the trend, stamp out selfishness, and convince others that they *can* make a difference. They have no political power and don't want it. They don't believe in marches or demonstrations. They don't have advanced degrees in political science or sociology. They are simply one couple—a sixth-grade teacher and a social worker— who have taken their Christian commitment seriously. They have found that giving is rewarding and that, even in a country of 200 million, it is possible to have an impact.

"We have to revive the individual's belief in his own responsibility," Joe Ann emphasizes. "We need people who are totally committed to the task of helping others. This is what it will take to wipe out poverty. We know it won't happen today or tomorrow. We may have to die before our philosophy is fully accepted. But we believe it can be done."

*I had never met anyone like Joe Ann
and Monroe. They showed me what a
thrilling experience it is to help somebody
else.*

— JOAN BROWN

12

CARING IS CONTAGIOUS

The Ballards have discovered that the best way to communicate their beliefs about helping is through their extended family. Young people who come to them for help and advice often develop a strong desire to help others.

This happened to Tom, one of the teenagers whom the Ballards assisted. He determined to help a crippled, old man who lived nearby. But the old man was a little suspicious at first. He had seen enough television news reports and read enough grisly newspaper stories to be wary of teenage boys.

Imagine his shock one afternoon when he found Tom at his door. "Maybe I could help you clean your house," the youth suggested hopefully. "Maybe I could do some errands for you since you don't get around so good."

In spite of his suspicion, Tom finally convinced the old man he really did want to help him. He cleaned his house and ran a few errands for him. But the old man insisted on paying him for the work.

"I took the money and bought him some groceries," Tom recalled. "When he saw all the food, he started crying. I reminded him that it was my money and that was the way I wanted to spend it."

Several years before, the youth wouldn't have given the old man a second thought. He was tied up in his own difficulties. When he was twelve, his home burned to the ground. Then he struggled through the battles of his parents, the early pregnancies of his two teenage sisters, and the daily problem of poverty. He would probably have been fighting on the streets if the Ballards hadn't given him a helping hand.

After his life stabilized, he developed an abiding desire—as have other Ballard young people—to share with others. He gave his best pair of pants to a schoolmate so the boy would have something to wear to church. On another occasion he and another boy chased a thief and retrieved a woman's stolen purse.

This same desire to help motivated Karice and Anna to show other potential students how to get financial aid for college. It persuaded Lisa to prepare for a career working with troubled juveniles. It made Alison reach out to kids at her husband's church. It sent Gladys Generette to Africa and the Dominican Republic as a missionary. It persuaded Eric to become a minister—one who would always have time for young people.

These young adults echo each other in speaking of the growing generosity they feel toward other people:

Alison: "A lot of times you want to help people, but you just don't know how to go about doing it. Monroe and Joe Ann taught me how."

Eric: "There are so many who need help these days. They don't have a home or they're hooked on drugs or alcohol. They need someone to talk with them and help them out. When I'm older, I'm going to help young people like Monroe and Joe Ann helped me."

Karice: "Because the Ballards have helped me, I want to help others. I would like to tell people, 'Don't give up. You can make it if you keep trying.' "

Lisa: "I want to help people the way Brother Monroe and Sister Joe helped me. I want to be the kind of person who cares about others."

Naturally, such responses are pleasing to the couple. In addition to putting these young people on their feet, they have started a chain reaction of neighborliness. After watching Anna pack a box of clothes for another church member one day, Joe Ann smiled. "Young people learn how they can help others by watching us. Someone else might have thrown those clothes away, but Anna knew to give them to someone who can use them."

Adults are also influenced by the Ballards' work. Their spirit of giving seems to bring out the best in other people.

A wealthy citizen of Memphis donates $2,000 for Christmas gifts for their young people each year. Several churches donated clothing, shoes, sheets, and money to help send Alison to college. A department store manager sold them a wedding dress well below the wholesale price for Alison's wedding. A motel gave their foster daughters free rooms during the weekend of Monroe's family reunion. A dairyman sends dairy products and orange juice that can no longer be sold in the stores. Vegetable markets contribute slightly bruised bushels of produce. Businessmen all over Memphis give clothes and other merchandise.

"She'll take anything, even though it looks unwearable," said Gerald Fried, a manager of a local department store. "I feel very good about helping." Other Memphis merchants express this same sentiment, and add that the Ballard example has heightened their own desire to do good works. At a branch of a well known retail store, E. E. Ferguson, supervisor of shipping and receiving, has been giving the Ballards damaged goods for longer than he can remember. He enjoys taking a part in their work. "I'm glad our store is doing this," he says. "The winters in Memphis get mighty cold. It's good to know you're helping keep some kids warm."

Men like Ferguson, Fried, and countless others are an integral part of the Ballards' domino theory of giving. Their unusual avocation is both dependent on the generosity of others and a catalyst for it.

Some of the adults assisted by the Ballards have started ministries similar to theirs. Although some of these have failed (see Chapter 7), others are now making important contributions to the community.

Joan Brown, a mother of four, first met Monroe when he and his brother Sylvester were knocking on doors in the neighborhood, inviting people to church. At the time, she had reached a low point in her life. Without a formal education, she couldn't find a job. Her marriage was in trouble. She had nothing to do except care for her children and wallow in her own dark moods. She wasn't interested in attending church, but she agreed to send her children on Sundays. Soon, seeing the youngsters' enthusiasm, she started going herself.

Her initial reluctance is difficult for people to believe now when they see her driving the church bus, working with children in Sunday School, and taking eight or nine kids home for Sunday dinner twice a month. "I had never met anyone like Joe Ann and Monroe before," she explains. "They showed me what a thrilling experience it is to help somebody else."

Before Joan Brown started working with young people in her home, Joe Ann helped her with some of her difficulties. She encouraged her to get a learner's permit, then a driver's license. She helped her find a job working with elderly residents in public housing. She had her utilities turned back on, then arranged a workable schedule to pay the overdue bills.

Joan is now helping other people with their utility problems. She has a job supervising the distribution of nutritious food to people in housing projects. Studying for a degree in accounting, she has big plans to help young people. "A lot of these kids just don't know there's a better way," she said. "My goal is to help them break out of ghetto living and build a bright future for themselves."

The Ballards' influence on their friends and neighbors proves it's possible to motivate people to help others. "When people see you doing something like this, they want to help too," said Joe Ann, her deep voice soft and earnest. Nothing is more important to her than enlisting others in this effort.

But the Ballards want to reach more people—those who can't see the work firsthand—the multitudes who live outside their neighborhood, beyond Memphis and Tennessee. "We can influence the people right around us, but what about the millions who have forgotten the concept of caring for each other?" Joe Ann asked. "There's a lot of work to do and we'll never get it done with a handful of people."

This is why the Ballards are now trying to take their message to a broader audience. Recently they taught a seminar on "Helping Through Personal Involvement" at Shelby State Community College in Memphis. They have spoken at civic clubs, the PTA, numerous churches, sororities, and schools. They are also trying to reach people through newspapers, magazine articles, television programs, and, finally, this book.

"We're not writing a book to brag about our work," Monroe told one community agency. "We hope it will attract attention to the needs of mankind. We don't feel we should leave all the work like this to community agencies. Average, everyday people should be sharing the responsibility and the rewards."

This is the message that young friends of Joe Ann and Monroe have learned from their example. Sixteen-year-old Eric Wells puts it this way: "Anyone can help others. You don't have to have a million dollars to get involved with people. An ordinary person can do a lot if he just tries."

PART TWO

HOW TO GO ABOUT DOING GOOD

In a wide-ranging interview that covers everything from their marriage to their views on discipline, the Ballards reveal the attitudes and values that have motivated their ministry. They offer practical suggestions for practicing love and caring sensibly and effectively.

I

SHARING: A FAMILY AFFAIR

Q. How do your own three children react to your work?

> **A.** They're really not too concerned about it now because they're still quite young. Anyway, they get a lot of attention from the young people who live with us. These kids are usually quite a bit older than our own children. They fuss over the little ones and do things for them. Our biggest worry is that our children may be getting spoiled by all the attention!

Q. Do you anticipate problems when they're older?

> **A.** We do have some concern about that. In another year or so, it could present problems for Ephie, our oldest. Before she starts resenting the situation, we plan to make some changes in our operation. When she's a teenager, we'll probably stop taking teenagers into the house to live. Then we'll work more with younger children. We think it's a good idea to keep a wide age range between our children and those we are helping. This should help to keep down the competition.

Q. What else do you do to make sure your own children aren't neglected?

A. It's true that our family is extended to include more people, but we probably spend more time together than most families. We're always home at night with the children. And on Saturdays and Sundays, we plan activities together.

We try to make sure that we don't sacrifice anything that our own children really need or want. We give up such things as fancy cars or outside entertainment that might be detrimental to them anyway.

We also make it a point to meet the small needs of our children immediately. If Monroe Jr.'s tricycle breaks, we try to fix it right away. You can always make time for little projects like that. They mean a lot to a child. We don't want them to think, *Mama and Daddy care more about other people's problems than mine.*

Q. Many parents would be afraid to bring children from such severely deprived environments into their home. Aren't you concerned that the bad habits and values of these kids might rub off on your own children?

A. Not really. We try to avoid that problem by helping children who are older than our own and by resisting the temptation to make them baby-sitters. It would be easy to ask these older boys and girls to stay with our little ones. But we are always around to keep a watchful eye on what is going on. Our weekend visitors

don't get a chance to pass on their street-
wise ways to our children.

Q. Where do you get the energy to do so much?

A. It's a way of life for us. You grow into
an attitude of *doing*. Maybe it's something
you learn. We condition ourselves to get
certain things done. We don't give up and
relax until they're accomplished. Some
people have a negative attitude about any
kind of work. They groan and moan
about "blue Monday," and they can't wait
until the weekend.

Most of our days are very full. We get
up at about 6:30. Once we eat breakfast,
we're ready to go—either to our jobs or to
some other activity. Sitting around doing
nothing isn't our style. But some people
make idleness and inactivity their highest
goal in life. They think you're crazy if you
like to be busy.

Q. Do you ever set aside time just for yourselves as a
couple?

A. We're together a lot, although there
are usually other people around. Once
we went away for Thanksgiving to
celebrate our anniversary. But that was
only once in the eleven years since Ephie
was born. We just don't like being away
from our children.

Q. How do you avoid feeling burdened and resentful
of all the responsibility?

A. If we took time to think about it, we

probably would feel burdened! We ask God regularly to bear us up and help us handle it. Jesus said, "When you pray and ask for something, believe that you have received it, and you will be given whatever you ask for" (Mark 11:24, TEV). Instead of feeling the responsibility ourselves, we put it in God's hands. We find great strength in prayer. Sometimes, we are completely exhausted at the end of the day. These are the times when we really have to ask God to renew our strength.

Q. Practically speaking, when you are dealing with so many people and so many problems, how do you keep everything straight?

A. It helps to take one problem at a time. Sometimes we have so many things to do that we don't know where to start. That's frustrating. We've discovered it's best to pick out one thing at a time and concentrate on that until it's done.

Q. In the twelve years of your marriage, have you ever wished for some luxuries that you wouldn't allow yourself to have?

A. If we ever had that desire, we have worn it out by now! We just can't think of anything we really need that we don't have. What we have is such an improvement over what we grew up with. We don't have to get up and put wood on the fire. We have an electric heater, an air conditioner, and a stove. Our refrigerator makes ice so we don't have to bother with the iceman. We're satisfied.

We don't have any desire for fancy, expensive clothes because we like to work too much and we can't work very well in clothes like that. It's not our style to spend money on fancy cars or luxury vactions. We could never feel right about spending a lot of money on those things.

Q. How do you keep from getting your feelings hurt at times when you receive criticism or when you try to be helpful and people don't respond?

A. We support each other. And if we feel good about our work, it really doesn't matter what other people think. You have to do this kind of work without expecting praise from others. We are secure in the belief that we're working for others, not for ourselves.

We haven't always had this philosophy. In the early years we often got upset by what someone said. Or we'd be afraid to help a person because someone might criticize. But we have overcome that fear through the years.

Q. Don't you get depressed sometimes over the problems you encounter?

A. No. We see so many positive results from our efforts. Even if we're having real problems with one child, we can look back and see the progress other kids have made. Problems are depressing only when people have no hope of working them out.

II

TIPS FOR HELPING TROUBLED YOUNGSTERS

Q. What are the most common mistakes adults make in dealing with children?

> **A.** The biggest mistake is to deal with the child's obvious problem instead of trying to discover what's causing the problem. Let's say a boy is having trouble in school. It could be that he's living in such a bad home environment that he can't study. Or his parents might be fighting all the time. But most adults deal with the surface difficulty. They don't try to find out why this boy is having problems in school.
>
> Another big mistake is to treat kids, especially underprivileged children, too gently. Most of these children need a firm hand. An adult should never accept a child's bad behavior without trying to understand the reasons behind it.

Q. How do you maintain order and discipline when you have so many children in your home at the same time?

> **A.** Discipline is not a one-shot deal. It's more of a system with us. We have established a kind of environmental control in this house. The children realize

from the very beginning that they can't get by with bad behavior. They don't curse or act disrespectful or destructive. Newcomers see other children acting with respect, and they follow that model.

Q. But how did you establish that kind of control?

A. For one thing, we're consistent. We make sure that our rules are always applied in the same way. For example, if you want a child to stay in his seat until a meal is finished, you can't let him leave the table one time and not the next. This confuses the child. You have to be consistent in what you expect of him.

Q. You also have rules to help you maintain discipline. What are they?

A. Our rules are pretty simple. We don't tolerate drinking, smoking, or cursing in our home. Girls must wear dresses because we feel they are more feminine and less suggestive than pants. Those young people who live with us must tell us where they are going when they leave the house and they have to be home at a reasonable hour. Although we have some basic rules for everyone, we always try to deal with people as individuals. A rule of not going out in the evening, for example, might be appropriate for one teenager and not for another.

Q. Some critics might charge that rules like these are too demanding and authoritarian.

A. Our rules help define our beliefs, and they let young people know where we stand. We recognize that people have a right to disagree with our rules and live their own lives. But if a child is in our house, we insist that he follow our instructions. Most adults don't communicate their beliefs strongly enough to children. They're afraid they might alienate them or lose their trust.

Q. How *do* you get and keep their trust?

A. A child will trust when he knows what to expect. We try to be consistent and keep our promises. If we promise to take a child out to dinner or to buy him a radio, we follow through. When we are dealing with a child whose trust level is very low, we do things with quick returns in our first contacts.

It's also important for a child to know that we demand nothing in return for our love. So many of the children we deal with are accustomed to paying for the love they get. This makes them very suspicious. So we try to let them know that we love them with no strings attached.

Q. Why do some adults have so much trouble communicating with children?

A. They don't realize that children can be very literal-minded. They take idle remarks or promises seriously. If a parent says, "We don't have any money to pay this bill," the children may start worrying that the family is really destitute. In communicating with children, we make sure we say what we mean and mean what we say.

Q. How do children react when they find out about your rules?

A. Some children resent them at first. But they soon discover that rules can bring order and security into their lives. I remember one girl who complained about how dull it was at our house and how restrictive the rules were. But she kept coming back every weekend. Our rules brought some peace and order into her life.

Q. What happens when someone breaks a rule?

A. Actually, we have had very few rules broken in this house. We keep a close watch on the behavior of the kids. If we see one who is headed for trouble, we talk with him before his behavior gets out of hand. So many of our young people believe in keeping the rules that a rule-breaker doesn't get much support from the rest of the group. When someone breaks a rule, a simple reprimand is usually all that is necessary. Sometimes we have to ask a person to give some thought to his conduct before he joins in our activities. When he apologizes he then rejoins the group and nothing else is said.

Q. Have you ever found it necessary to forbid someone to come to your house?

> **A.** Yes. I remember one girl who stole
> some cosmetics, then lied about taking
> them. As punishment, we told her not to
> come back the next weekend. About a
> week later she apologized and we were
> glad to have her back.

Q. These kids obviously enjoy visiting with both of
you. What attracts them to your home?

> **A.** For starters, they know there is
> always something to eat. They have also
> learned that we'll get them clothes to
> wear and see about their other material
> needs. But maybe the most important
> reason is that we take their problems
> seriously. Their problems might seem silly
> to other adults, but we remember what it
> was like to be young. Maybe we are still
> living out our own childhood in some
> ways. We like to be around children—to
> play games with them and tell stories and
> visit the places they enjoy. We like to
> have fun, and they always seem to have
> fun when they're with us.

Q. Do you have planned activities for youngsters
when they visit?

> **A.** We always keep materials on hand
> for them to use or play with. Or we may
> decide to have a picnic, fly kites together,
> or let them help us sort the donated
> clothes that we pick up from the stores.
> We show them, too, that quiet, low-key

activities can also be a lot of fun. We don't allow them to play baseball or basketball around the house on Sunday. This should be a quiet, thoughtful time.

Q. How do you help these children with their material needs?

A. For one thing, we help provide their school clothing. Many parents call each fall to request clothes and shoes for their kids. They think of us almost as a department store. We give food too, if we're asked. But food isn't as big a problem today as it used to be. Most needy families can qualify for food stamps and other forms of institutional assistance.

Q. How do you prevent a child from taking advantage of you?

A. In most cases, we don't try. We realize that we "took advantage" of our own parents by expecting them to feed us, keep us warm, clothe us, or help us solve our problems. That's what parents are for. We want children to feel that we are their "parents" while they are in our home. We hope they will learn some positive values like honesty, unselfishness, and respect for others.

Q. Isn't there a danger they'll become dependent on you?

A. We try to make it clear that children should set their own goals so they can eventually take care of themselves. While we're giving away clothing or taking a child to dinner, we're also training him. There's nothing wrong with receiving from others, but we also teach them to provide for themselves.

Some people wonder about our policy of encouraging some kids to stay in our home even after they have finished college. We feel that this practice actually fosters independence, because this allows these young adults to save some money and really be able to stand on their own feet when they get out on their own. The young people know that our goal is to help them so they *can* be independent.

Q. But what if one of these kids started spending money on fancy clothes or bought an expensive car?

A. This would tell us that he really didn't need us and he would have to find a place of his own. Fortunately, we haven't had this problem.

The young women who are living with us now are saving some money toward the day when they can be totally on their own. The reason college graduates continue to live with us is so they can put away their own money for a better future. If a person at this stage of life should feel that he doesn't need to save, he doesn't belong here.

Q. Do you expect anything else from the young people you help?

A. Respect—and that's about all. They

don't owe us anything—not money, not work, not even thanks. People have a hard time understanding this. But our ministry is for the benefit of these young people—not to boost our egos.

Q. Have you ever failed to get respect from any of the kids?

A. Not really. Of course, we have encountered some who were rude or unpleasant. But we expect a certain amount of backtalk or rudeness. Obviously, these children haven't been taught the finer points of etiquette.

Q. Do their parents usually support you in your work?

A. Yes, almost always. Many of these parents can't deal successfully with their children's problems, and they're grateful for our help. As we get to know the children, we try to determine if the parents need our assistance in other ways.

Q. Don't parents get jealous of your relationship with their children?

A. Not often. Sadly, most parents don't seem to care what we do with their children. Jealousy is more likely to crop up because of the progress the child is making. Some parents are afraid their children will become superior to them. This attitude has slowed our progress occasionally.

Q. The young women living with you now are in their early twenties. When does a child become an adult?

A. A child is not automatically an adult when he reaches the age of eighteen or twenty-one or twenty-five, but when he becomes mature enough to make decisions for himself. Many young people have the attitude that reaching adulthood gives you license to do all kinds of forbidden things. We try to teach our children to do what's right, whatever their age.

Too much emphasis is placed on the number of years a person has lived. Legally, a person is considered an adult at age eighteen by most states. But at this age he may be far from ready to take care of himself. If a person has the attitude, *I'm grown and you can't tell me anything,* then he has shut himself off from any future growth.

III

THE BALLARDS' POVERTY PROGRAM

Q. In your opinion, what are the most pressing needs of the poor?

A. Jobs, food, housing, unstable family life, and poor education—all these are pressing needs. But the biggest problem we've found is a self-defeating attitude and a lack of positive values among the poor. Even with all the assistance available, this problem is seldom addressed. If a person doesn't want to do better and improve his life, he won't be able to keep a job, take care of his house, or bring up his children right. A bad attitude coupled with a lack of values leaves a person in a desperate situation.

Q. You don't feel that material needs are the most pressing problem among the poor?

A. Probably the poor people themselves think so. Perhaps the public does too. But from our point of view, it has to be values. If you don't teach a person how to live and take care of himself, then you're wasting your time if you give him nothing more than goods. The people we help actually live in our house. We teach them values by example.

Q. What specific values are you talking about?

A. Knowing how to get the maximum use out of things. Caring about what happens to yourself and others. Working for what you want out of life. Planning for your future. Learning to say no to destructive habits like drinking, partying, and gambling. Realizing the power within yourself to change your situation. Not spending foolishly. We know some people who are deeply in debt. But when they get a few extra dollars, they don't think of paying those bills—they immediately buy something frivolous.

Q. How do you explain such irresponsibility?

A. Many of the people trapped in poverty think only about the here and now. They're convinced they have no future, so tomorrow doesn't concern them. We've seen welfare mothers put down fifteen dollars for a pair of shoes on layaway. Then they have to do without groceries the next month to finish paying for them. This is what happens when "looking good" today becomes the highest goal in life.

Q. Some people get very edgy when you talk about teaching your values to somebody else. Do you see any problem with this?

A. No. We don't insist that our values be accepted absolutely by everyone. But we do have a set of values that some poor people have never been exposed to. If they see that our system works, then they have a choice they never had before. You can't choose a different life unless you know what that way of life has to offer.

Q. Are you able to make people understand that they do have a choice—that they can have a better life?

A. Some people will never believe that they can do anything for themselves. They sell themselves short. But many *will* listen—especially young people. On the surface they may have defeatist attitudes. But these aren't ingrained as deeply as those of their parents.

Q. What are some of these young people like when they first come to you?

A. They're selfish. They want the best of everything. Most of them have little self-control. They'll walk out a door and let it slam behind them on someone else. This says a lot about their attitude toward others. They shut themselves off from other people.

Q. The way some of these kids grow up, isn't it understandable why they would shut themselves off from people?

A. Yes. And that's very dangerous. After doing this for a while, they may not value anything—even life. We had to start with Lisa and Alison at base zero and teach them just about everything—to care about each other, to care about cleanliness, to care about other people.

In their first few weeks with us, their standard response was "I don't care." They had lost the ability to feel deeply about anything.

Q. After you reach a person and his negative attitude begins to change, what else can you do to help him out of the poverty rut?

A. We can't do much about housing, but we encourage people to look for better places to live. Living in a hot, crowded, dirty little shack takes its toll on spirit and energy. It breeds irritability. It can cause apathy and negligence in children. A child cannot get rested enough in conditions like these to do good work in school.

Q. What about education? How does it fit into your philosophy of helping people?

A. A lot of kids from the ghetto just don't see any purpose in going to school because their parents don't care about it. The children aren't dumb; the parents are negligent. But the kids who live at our house have to go to school and get an education. There's no question about it. Education can help a person pull himself out of poverty. If he can get an education, he should be capable of finding and holding a job.

Q. Why do some young people give up so easily on their education? Don't they realize it's important?

A. They just don't get enough encouragement. This problem is prevalent among black people who have developed the attitude that they need nothing more than an eighth grade or maybe a high school education. We hear a lot of mothers say, "I'm going to get my kids through the twelfth grade—and that's all." Their own parents taught them that education wasn't important because black people couldn't get better jobs anyway. That's not true anymore, but the attitude lives on.

In some families, a single child may decide he wants to go to college. But the others often try to talk him out of it. They'll do everything they can to keep him from going on to school. We can help in situations like this. By bringing that child into our home, we can give him the encouragement he needs to continue his schooling.

Q. You've helped hundreds of people get jobs. Why do they have trouble getting jobs on their own?

A. Many people won't agree with us on this. But we think it's because they don't really try to find jobs. They don't try because there's too much public assistance available. If you know that you can get by without working, then you don't bother about doing any better. If some demands were made on people who receive public assistance, their attitudes might change. Instead, the government seems to reward loose living. We know girls who get pregnant deliberately so they can receive the $100.00 monthly welfare check. They start getting the check when they're only four months pregnant.

Q. But don't you give people handouts too?

A. We don't give handouts—we give a hand up! As we give to people, we're also training them. It's clear to us and to them that the object of our giving is to help them become independent, not more dependent.

Q. But what about people who really do want to work? Are there other reasons why they have trouble finding jobs?

A. They might be too picky. Or they might not know how to act when they apply for jobs. They might be rude, sloppily dressed, or late for the interview.

Q. What advice would you give to applicants?

A. When we send a person out to look for a job, we tell him to dress neatly without overdressing; to appear confident but not cocky; and to get there on time. We've also found that it pays to have a respectful attitude.

Q. Are jobs available for the poor?

A. Plenty of them. We don't know what people mean when they say there are no jobs. We know companies that are severely understaffed because they can't find workers.

Q. Maybe you know where to look for jobs. Any tips?

A. We've discovered that an employment office isn't necessarily the best place. We go to big companies like trucking firms because they often have openings. We try to follow business trends and the job market so we know where the best openings might be.

Q. Let's talk about hunger for a moment. Even with food stamps and other types of assistance, is it true that some children in this city still go hungry?

A. Yes, because their parents sell the food stamps. Stamps are easily bought and sold. A lot of young people go without food or eat nothing but cookies and other snack foods every day. Alcohol is expensive, but a great many parents drink excessively. When they sell their food stamps and spend the money on whiskey, their children have to do without nutritious meals.

Q. Some people may have good motives. Could it be that they just aren't shopping intelligently?

A. That's right. They shop at the wrong stores. They go to the little corner convenience stores where everything is much more expensive. Or they'll always buy a name brand when a store brand gives the same quality at a lower price. They also buy a lot of expensive prepared foods such as instant potatoes, breaded shrimp, or sausage and biscuits. Some mothers buy a delicacy to suit their personal taste—maybe a can of pressed ham. This may be very tasty, but it won't stretch very far in a large family.

Q. How can we help parents give their children the food they need?

A. Food baskets and other types of short-term help go only so far. There is plenty of good, cheap food available if parents would take the time to find—and prepare it. We can help these parents and their children by trying to change their values and attitudes.

IV

PACKAGED CARING SERVICES

Q. How would you describe your relations with the organized social services in Memphis?

> **A.** We try to maintain good relations with them at all times, even though we don't always agree with their methods. You see, we often have to turn to them because we don't have the resources to handle all the problems we face.

Q. What kind of problems are you unable to handle by yourselves?

> **A.** We are aware of our limitations. If someone has a mental problem, we know he needs the attention of a trained therapist. If he's on drugs, we know he needs someone who is trained to handle that problem. Nor are we qualified to give legal advice, so we help the person needing a lawyer to find good legal assistance he can afford. Sometimes, a family will need long-term financial assistance. Although we can't actually give support ourselves, we can contact agencies that *will* help.

Q. The social service system can be confusing, especially to uneducated people who are in trouble.

Do you have any suggestions that would help people deal more successfully with agencies?

A. For people who need help, we believe it's very important to be honest. If social workers know they can trust you, they'll be much more willing to give aid. Often, poor people have an ineffective way of dealing with agencies. They're scared, or defensive, or embarrassed, and they may try to camouflage their *real* problem.

For those who try to find assistance for others, we think it's very important to start building personal contacts. If you have established good relationships in advance, you're more likely to get the help and cooperation you need. It is also advisable to get as much information as possible about each agency and the services it offers.

Q. No one really regulates your work. How do you regulate yourselves so that you stay within the law?

A. First of all, we generally don't have young people living with us under the legal age of eighteen. Younger children stay with us only temporarily. If they want to stay over on the weekends, we always get a note of permission from the parent or guardian. Legally, we are also forbidden to have more than a certain number of people stay with us at one time. So, we have to watch that. We have a lawyer who gives us free advice when legal questions come up and that's very helpful.

Q. Why won't you take a foster child from the welfare department or get more involved with organized social service programs?

> **A.** We would never accept money for caring for a child. The young people we help appreciate the fact that we're helping them because we love them—not because an agency is paying us to board them.
>
> We stay away from organized programs because we can't agree with all of their regulations. We prefer to follow our own guidelines.

Q. How do your regulations differ from their regulations?

> **A.** For one thing, agencies or the welfare department advise you to use behavior modification in solving problems with young people. They give all this psychological jargon and all these psychological tips for handling problems. We simply try to change a person's heart by showing that we care. We believe that if you change a person's heart, his attitudes and actions will change.
>
> Generally, we believe we're stricter than the welfare department. The welfare department might think that our rules are too restrictive, that they infringe on a child's "individual liberties." We believe our house rules help us teach values that will guide children all their lives.

V

HOW TO GIVE UNTIL IT HELPS

A. What kind of emotional qualifications does a person need to do what you're doing?

> **Q.** A deep love for people is essential. You have to be tough enough to take criticism and survive the times when things don't work right or your finances and energy run low. You need strong beliefs and firm conviction in God and in what you're doing.

Q. With the right motives and convictions, could *anyone* do this work?

> **A.** Anyone can do what we're doing if he's willing to develop a serving attitude. We had to make some changes in our lives in order to do this kind of work. It's just like going to school. You need the right attitude before you can study and learn. You have to be serious before you can live the kind of life that serves as an example for the people you help.

Q. What do you mean by serving as an example?

> **A.** We're talking about the kind of home life that you would want your children to imitate. If you don't want your children to drink or smoke, then you shouldn't drink

or smoke yourself. We know one couple who provides a home for foster sons. They seem to be doing a good job, but the father goes to the dog races all the time. What kind of example is that setting for these boys? A person who smokes, drinks, gambles, or uses profane language is not in a good position to tell a child what he should be doing with his life.

Q. You seem to fit so much into each day. Do you have any tips on time management?

A. Before you go to bed, think about what you need to do the next morning. It's a good idea to write it down. Then when you get up, you don't have to waste time thinking about what you should do next. A lot of people waste time running little errands because they are not organized. Organization brings peace of mind. Little details often make the difference between success and failure.

Q. It must take a lot of money to care for all these children. How do you manage so successfully?

A. The secret is to budget very carefully and avoid unnecessary expenses. We both work full-time, and occasionally take extra work to earn more.

Our combined $30,000 annual salary comes to about $1,900 a month after taxes. Of this amount, $150 goes for the payment on our motor home; $80 goes to a personal loan; $100 to a home improvement loan that enabled us to add the attic rooms and bathroom; $65, savings account; $15, an emergency transportation fund; $190, tithe to the church; $200, telephone and utility bills; $94, to the house note; we set aside $250 for food; and $250 meets the costs for daily transportation, clothing, and miscellaneous personal expenses. We use the remaining $500 to entertain the children, buy them little treats, and meet emergency needs.

Q. According to Department of Agriculture studies, a family of four spends almost $300 a month on food even if they're trying to economize. You're feeding at least nine people every day for less than that. How do you keep your costs so low?

A. We save a lot by buying in bulk. We are also very organized about how we spend our food money. We make one major trip to the grocery store each month, but we buy vegetables and fruits at a produce market that we visit regularly. We have two refrigerators and two freezers so we can buy in bulk and store the food until we need it.

We also save money by buying vegetables and fruit that are marked or bruised. Once we were able to buy a whole case of greens for $1.00, and half a bushel of tomatoes for just fifty cents. We have enough celery and bell peppers stored away to last a year. We grind these into pulp and juice, which we use for spaghetti and dressings. Sometimes, too, stores help us out by giving us surplus foods.

Q. You never know when you might have three or four or more guests for dinner. That uncertainty would drive most cooks wild. But you say you are always glad to feed anyone who drops in. How do you do it?

A. We always prepare some extra food, just in case. If no one comes by, we can always eat what's left over the next day.

Actually, we ourselves are sometimes puzzled by how it works out. It reminds us of the passage in Matthew that describes how Jesus fed the multitudes with five loaves and two pieces of fish. Sometimes we're certain we haven't cooked enough, but these are the times when we seem to have food left over. God seems to multiply what we have.

Q. Don't you ever have to throw some of this food out?

A. We don't allow waste. That's how we can get food to stretch so far. We tell the children that they can take what they want, but they must eat what they take. "Don't waste food," we tell them, "because what you throw away could have been used to feed one more person at this table. Or it could be used to keep you from going hungry tomorrow."

Q. Eliminating other waste in your home must be important in a ministry like this. How would you advise other people to economize?

A. The most important point is to stop wasting things yourself. And this means a lot of little things. Don't shake any amount of detergent into the washing machine when the directions call for a cup. Don't let the water run while brushing your teeth. Turn off the light or radio when leaving a room. Pick up your supplies in one trip to the store rather than making five separate trips. These might seem like insignificant things, but with many people in your house, the waste and expense really add up. You need to develop a habit of conservation in these little matters so others will follow your example.

Q. How do you draw the line between helping some-one and butting into his private life?

A. Usually, people will let you know if they want your help. You have to accept the fact that some suffering people just won't let you help them. They feel their problems are none of your business. You have no choice but to leave those people alone.

Q. Does it help to be persistent and keep offering?

A. Sometimes you just have to take the hint that you're not wanted. In other cases you may be able to do some good eventually if you're not too pushy about it. Sometimes an indirect approach is the best method. If you know a neighbor has serious financial difficulties, start out by

142/ROOM IN OUR HEARTS

offering just a little help. Tell him you have a pair of shoes that might fit his youngest son. If he's responsive to that, you can look for other discreet ways to help. This works much better than rushing in with the superior attitude that you're really going to help this poor old boy.

Q. How would you suggest that other people approach store owners and business people to ask for their help in a ministry like this?

A. First, you have to prove that you're honest. Most store owners will probably check with a neighbor or someone in the community to find out about you. Then, they'll give you more and more as you prove yourself. At least, that's how it has worked with us. Now they know that we'll cut the store labels and tags off their donated merchandise so people can't return them for a refund. They also know from experience that the poor people who need the goods are the ones who receive them. But it took time to win that trust.

Second, when you ask store owners for something for a specific purpose, make sure you use it in that way. And finally, keep good records that show what you're doing with donated materials. We keep a list of people who receive clothes, along with their addresses and telephone numbers. Most store owners have never asked to see it, but the fact that we have it probably makes them feel better about us.

Q. How did you get the word out about your ministry to so many people?

> **A.** At first, information spread through churches. After we established a good system and gained experience, we made a concerted effort to get publicity. News about us spread through articles in the local newspapers, television reports, and word of mouth. A library information referral service in Memphis also was a big help. Our names are on file there as resources for people who need clothes or families who may be wiped out by a fire or other disaster.

Q. What other suggestions would you give to people who want to start helping others?

> **A.** Start out by working with only a few people. Avoid the temptation to set ambitious goals for the first year. If you put a quota on what you ought to do or the amount of success or satisfaction you'll enjoy, you're only inviting defeat. Above all, start with the right motives. Do your work unselfishly, sacrificially, and tirelessly. Start slowly, be positive, and keep on—even in the face of discouragement.

THE DOOR IS ALWAYS OPEN . . .

As Joe Ann watched Anna and Karice receive their college diplomas on graduation day, her mind was churning with plans for the coming summer. She was five months pregnant and up for an important new job. Monroe was to start his own summer job the next day. And the two new graduates were eagerly waiting to step into the working world for the first time.

The hot summer proved to be as busy as she had expected. Joe Ann became director of the Northside Christian Center in Memphis, sponsored by Youth For Christ and Young Life. Karice and Anna continued living with the Ballards, but began an eighteen-month CETA stint, working in physical therapy for the handicapped. Lisa studied for her high school equivalency test in September, while her sister, Alison, returned to Texas, where her husband is now a pastor.

At home in the red brick house, life followed its usual course. There were Sunday dinners to share and visits from old friends and a yard that was frequently packed with a crowd of neighborhood children. On weekends and evenings in July, Monroe built a motorized merry-go-round for the children. On her lunch hours, Joe Ann drove to department stores in search of damaged goods. And every Wednesday, Friday, and Sunday, the family went to church.

But the summer also brought tragedy. In August, Joe Ann delivered a stillborn baby. Emotionally and physically drained, she stayed in the hospital eight days. After learning that the stillborn birth and past miscarriages were due to a genetic problem, she and Monroe sadly decided to have no more children.

The loss of the infant was a crushing blow. Yet, as

146/ROOM IN OUR HEARTS

always, the Ballards felt blessed with the children they have and with the many young people who continue to enter their lives.

As they have shown so many times before, troubles do not stop them—or even slow them down for long. The couple knows that there are always children who need love, adults who need help, young people who need encouragement.

When the summer ended and the leaves began to turn, Monroe packed the motor home with the clothes, clean notebooks and unopened texts of two college freshmen. With the young women, their mothers, and some close friends, he drove two hundred miles to the same Nashville college where the Ballards had so happily observed the graduation ceremonies three months before.

It was time once again for the fall term . . . time for two more young women to find a future more hopeful than their past.

1 2 3 4 5 6 7 8 9 10 11 12 13 14 15 16 17